SIS, COMPLAINING IS REMAINING IN TOXIC THINKING

CHRISTIAN WOMEN CONQUERING NEGATIVE THOUGHTS AND EMOTIONS WHILE DEVELOPING WISDOM AND KNOWLEDGE TO OVERCOME SINFUL ACTIONS

MIA FARRAH

UNMERITED FAVOUR LLC

COPYRIGHT

© **Copyright** _____ 2022 - **All rights reserved.**

The content contained within this book may not be reproduced, duplicated or transmitted without direct written permission from the author or the publisher.Under no circumstances will any blame or legal responsibility be held against the publisher, or author, for any damages, reparation, or monetary loss due to the information contained within this book. Either directly or indirectly. You are responsible for your own choices, actions, and results.

Legal Notice: This book is copyright protected. This book is only for personal use. You cannot amend, distribute, sell, use, quote or paraphrase any part, or the content within this book, without the consent of the author or publisher.

Disclaimer Notice: Please note the information contained within this document is for educational and entertainment purposes only. All effort has been executed to present accurate, up to date, and reliable, complete information. No warranties of any kind are declared or implied. Readers acknowledge that the author is not engaging in the rendering of legal, financial, medical or professional advice. The content within this book has been derived from various sources. Please consult a licensed professional before attempting any techniques outlined in this book.

By reading this document, the reader agrees that under no circumstances is the author responsible for any losses, direct or indirect, which are incurred as a result of the use of the information contained within this document, including, but not limited to, — errors, omissions, or inaccuracies.

TABLE OF CONTENTS
Introduction 3
THE OUTRAGEOUS LIAR 3
Chapter-1 8
THE TOXICITY OF CHRONIC COMPLAINING 8
Chapter-2 18
YOUR THOUGHT LIFE 18
Chapter-3 27
THE PATTERNS THAT KEEP YOU STUCK 27
Chapter-4 37
RENEWAL – CONQUERING NEGATIVE THOUGHT 37
Chapter-5 51
TRANSFORM WHAT YOU SAY GOD'S WAY 51
Chapter-6 63
THE EMOTIONAL BEING IN YOU 63
Chapter-7 76
CULTIVATING GODLY GRATITUDE 76
Chapter-8 86
FINDING GOD IN TIMES OF CRISIS 86
Conclusion 97
THE BEST IS YET TO COME 97

Just for you!

An enlightening ebook that will give you a new revelation about the power of the Holy Communion! Download it right away!

Visit this link: unmeritedfavourllc.com

DEDICATION

Addison Grace Newsome,
My beautiful, courageous, and sweet niece who taught us that God is in control of life at all times. She fought the good fight and is now in the arms of Jesus. Heaven's gain is earth's loss. You will forever live in our hearts. Until we meet again, my sweetheart!

March 28, 2017 - October 22, 2021

INTRODUCTION

THE OUTRAGEOUS LIAR

In his letters to his nephew Wormwood, the demon Screwtape talks about his nephew's current victim by saying,

> *"We want him to be in the maximum uncertainty so that his mind will be filled with contradictory pictures of the future, every one of which arouses hope or fear. There is nothing like suspense and anxiety for barricading a human's mind against the Enemy. He wants men to be concerned with what they do; our business is to keep them thinking about what will happen to them."*
>
> — C.S. LEWIS

The senior demon was advising his nephew on dealing with a human who had been called to serve in the military. God wants human beings to focus on the present by standing on His promises. The Lord will lead us through every day because He is our Father. But the demon wants his nephew to entice and compel the victim into uncertainty. By filling the victim's mind with many contradictory pictures, he wants to create a sense of fear and anxiety in him.

The victim will think about the possibilities or outcomes of his military service due to the lies fed into his mind. He is going to spiral into a vicious cycle of anxiety and negative thinking because he assumes multiple outcomes. Fear is of the devil; it is not of God. Wormwood was advised to divert the victim from the present and shift his focus to the future. The devil often ushers us into unnecessarily thinking about our future or current situations' worst possible outcomes. He manipulates us into dreading the most hypothetical of outcomes. The devil loves making us his captives; he gains such pleasure by doing this. But let me tell you this,

THE DEVIL IS AN OUTRAGEOUS LIAR.

C.S. Lewis gives us a glimpse into the world of demons in his book, '*The Screwtape Letters*.' The devil is clearly very smart, dear friends. He is the greatest deceiver of all time. He has had centuries and centuries of practice, and he is a smooth liar. He is the accuser of the brethren and will do anything to separate us from God. But God is for us, and nothing can ever separate us from the love of God (Romans 8:38). Unfortunately, many of us fall prey to the devil's deception and his many tactics. God is ultimate, and He always has the last word. God wants us to focus on the present. We are His children, and He loves us with everlasting love. Our future is secure in Him. Jesus Christ holds you, dear friend. He will never leave you nor forsake you.

YOU ARE A CHILD OF GOD.

Your identity lies in Christ alone.

Do you believe everything you hear?

Have you ever tuned into the news and heard something crazy? Remember when people went crazy over the 2012 prophecy that the world would end? An ancient Mayan prophecy stated that the world would end on 21st December

INTRODUCTION

2012. The heathen prophecy was hyped to such a degree that a blockbuster movie was filmed on it. Doesn't this sound crazy? Well, it sure does to me!

Let me ask if you've ever heard a lie like this on the news or through a friend? Would you believe it? Do you believe everything that comes across your television screen or pops up on your computer? So there are many lies spread across the media and everywhere in general that it is difficult to separate fact from fiction at times.

Are you careful of what you let into your mind? What kind of thoughts do you entertain? A lot of fluff or information out there has no business being in your mind. The logical thing to do is to filter every thought that enters our minds. An average person thinks around 60,000 to 80,000 thoughts every day. Applying logic and filtering every single one of these thoughts is almost impossible, isn't it?

As believers, we are called to think the right things by 'testing' and 'approving' of what God wants us to think and do. Now the question that arises is, how do we do this? If we focus on unwholesome thoughts, we forfeit the ability to discern the will of God rightly. To test and approve a thought, you must evaluate it in the light of God's word. Has God given you a promise or a revelation? Is this thought shadowed by God's promise or revelation? If either does not approve of the thought, close it out. Cut it at the root before it grows larger.

The Bible says in 2 Corinthians 10:5, "We take captive every thought to make it obedient to Christ." How do we do this? We read the word of God daily, but do we apply it in our lives? Are we practicing our faith? The thoughts we have define our life. Are you letting your thoughts dictate your life?

The Apostle Paul says in Romans 12:2, "Do not conform to the pattern of this world, but be transformed by the

INTRODUCTION

renewing of your mind. Then you will be able to test and approve what God's will is - His good, pleasing and perfect will." Has the renewing of your mind transformed you? We are new creations in Christ Jesus, and our minds have been renewed by Him, but are we practicing this renewal?

The mundaneness of every day can get a bit too much at times. All of us are prone to fear; we aren't immune to it. But God has not given us a spirit of fear and timidity, but of power, love, and self-discipline (2 Timothy 1:7). So how do we embrace the power, love, and self-discipline that God gave us? I'll be honest here and tell you that I struggle with fear too. I exercise my right (the promise of being a child of God) as much as possible, but I have vulnerable days too.

I want you to be honest with yourself. What fear have you been struggling with? Is it the fear of losing someone? Is it the fear of never being 'good enough?' Is it the fear of being alone? Do you struggle with loneliness? Do you fear losing your money? Are you constantly worried about your child's health? Do you dread the future? I have some days where I struggle with fear of the future. I mean, But we are human at the end of the day.

With the recent pandemic, many of us have faced harsh circumstances. Many have lost their loved ones. Few of us have gone financially bankrupt. With the unsettling times that have fallen upon us, our minds are bound to be exposed to the worries of the days. Have you found yourself struggling with excessive anxiety? Have you been viewing things in a negative light for a long time? If you're struggling to find answers, this book is for you, dear friend. If you've tried time and again, yet you fail, read on. If you're looking for practical applications of the scriptures and a solution that is based on God's everlasting word, you are in the right place.

I have struggled with negative thoughts over and over again. I tried to get rid of them in my own strength, but we can shun these thoughts only by God's word. I have seen God's word change my thought life completely. There is massive, life-changing power in the name of Jesus! He renewed my mind, and He can renew yours too!

The Word of God has to be claimed and applied to change our thought patterns. Then, you can completely turn your mind over from negative to positive. You can conquer your fears, doubts, and anxieties. The devil is a liar, and you no longer have to believe his lies. Christ died and rose again for you and me. You can be free. He has already won the victory. Our job as believers is to live in His victory.

Jesus is the Prince of Peace and wants you to live in this peace. Before I sleep, I thank the Lord for the day and then tell Him that I rest in His love and peace. God wants you to live an abundant life filled with well-being and health in His Spirit. You matter to God, and He is calling you to live in His complete victory.

In this book, you will learn to examine your thought life and the patterns that keep you stuck. You will learn practical ways of conquering these negative thoughts plaguing your mind. You learn to transform and renew your mind using the word of God. Your thoughts matter to Him. You can win the battle for your mind. If you are engaged in a fight against negativity, this book will be your resource strategy to bring victory to you!

1

THE TOXICITY OF CHRONIC COMPLAINING

"For although they knew God, they did not honor him as God or give thanks to him, but they became futile in their thinking, and their foolish hearts were darkened."

— -ROMANS 1:21

I found myself anxious on busy workdays. So I decided to read an encouraging blog when I stumbled across something that Charles Spurgeon said: "As long as man is alive and out of hell, he cannot have any cause to complain." This caught me off-guard in a season of deep anxiety and trouble. I read my Bible and prayed every day, attended church every Sunday, and was a strong Christian, but my life felt like a disaster, and I couldn't seem to catch a break. Why was my life like this when I did everything to please God and follow His commands? I often found myself lost in thought, and the negativity crept in. As I read what Charles Spurgeon said, I felt the hot embers of guilt touching my heart. I was guilty of complaining, time and again. I was guilty of not practicing gratitude. I was guilty of being a grumbler.

Have you ever found yourself in an almost impossible situation where life does not seem fair? You're a Christian, and you know that God is over all things. You also understand that all things work out for good for those who trust Him, but you've struggled to surrender everything to Him. You start the day with a positive mindset yet struggle to carry the victory over your mind through the day. The negativity slips in, and by the time you realize it, you're already mounting up the complaints. The Christian life is war, and we know this because the Apostle Paul speaks of it in Ephesians 6:12, where he says that we battle the evil rulers and authorities of the unseen spiritual world and not mere flesh and blood. The struggle is real, and I know that the process of submitting to God in all areas of your life is very hard, but let me tell you that it is possible. To understand what the Bible says about complaining, let us dwell on its origins for a while here.

The Origins:

The word '*complain*' is derived from the Latin word '*complangere*,' which means bewail or lament or find fault. The Greek translation gives us four different meanings and instances where the word complain was used in the Bible. The first word is '*diaballo,*' which means 'to bring charges with a hostile intent' or 'to complain of.' An example of this can be seen in 1 Timothy 3:11, where women are called to be temperate and trustworthy, not malicious talkers. We are called women of God to despise negative talk because it dishonors God. The second word is '*diagogguzo,*' which means to 'murmur,' ' grumble,' or 'heavily complain.' The Israelites constantly grumbled and complained even though the Lord had always taken care of them, as seen in Exodus 16:2 and Numbers 14:2. The third word is '*talaiporeo,*' which means 'to suffer hardship' or 'be miserable' or 'to be beaten down.' An honest reaction to suffering hardships is lamenting, and we can see this in the life of Job. The fourth word is *'stenazo,'* which means 'to groan.' Paul says in 2 Corinthians 5:2, "For in this we groan, earnestly desiring to be clothed upon with our house which is from heaven." As believers, we are all groaning as we wait for our eternal redemption, for the time that Christ will take us home forever. Do you see how the first two types of complaining are very toxic? In contrast, the third and fourth types are genuine reactions where faith is applied and God is glorified.

The first complaint was seen in the book of Genesis when Adam said to God, "The woman whom you gave to be with me, she gave me fruit of the tree, and I ate." Adam blamed Eve for the sin that they both committed instead of repenting of what he did. Cain, the son of Adam, put out the second complaint ever recorded. The Bible records the rawest moments of various characters where they lamented or cried out to God through their hardships. Releasing our worries to God is fine and let me add to this and say that it is our responsibility, as children of God, to release our concerns to God. In fact, Jesus came to give us a garment of praise instead of a spirit of despair (Isaiah 60:3). He calls out to the weary and promises rest, and trust me, Sis, His rest is all you need because it is something the world can never give.

Complaining thwarts our peace and joy, and this is not good because Jesus is the Prince of Peace and the joy of the Lord is our strength. Do you see how complaining steals the blessings of God in the most silent of places? It is destructive and faithless complaining, or grumbling is a sin against God, as we see in the case of the Israelites in the wilderness. Complaining about God and worrying, forgetting to trust God's plan, or constantly grumbling is not right. Let me emphasize that chronic complaining is not soulful; it is not suitable for the human soul. When you frequently complain, you defy God's higher plans and choose not to trust His promises. Such a complaint can be seen in the book of Exodus 3, where God spoke to Moses through the burning bush, and despite God's constant reassurances, Moses kept making excuses. He chooses to rely on his circumstances rather than take refuge in the promises of God.

Complaining vs. Venting:

There is a distinct difference between complaining and venting. Venting involves trusting God and releasing one's emotions to Him knowing that He will be faithful through it all, whereas complaining ignores God's goodness and His character.

The Bible says that through many tribulations, we will enter the Kingdom of God (Acts 14:22). The Christian life is not easy, and I will tell you that you are not alone when you go through the many painful seasons of life. You have a companion, a faithful partner, and One who will never leave you nor forsake you through all of life's intense moments. Always remember that Jesus is standing right by your side through it all (Matthew 28:20).

To vent is to let out a trapped emotion. People vent under duress or stress as it helps release those emotions or express them, usually forcefully. A vent is an opening through which steam or air escapes, and it represents an outlet for these. Venting is known to reduce a person's stress levels and is a coping mechanism. Positive or faith-filled venting helps us calm down and return to rational thought. Our very human nature makes us fragile; therefore, we need to release our emotions from time to time as it is unhealthy to hoard them. Repressing one's emotions can be very harmful and leads to many emotional, mental, and physical problems. It is perfectly fine and healthy to vent. Maybe you've had a bad day at work, and now you just need to vent, or you've had a draining argument with a stranger, or it has just been one of those days where everything seems to go against the tide. Let me tell you, dear friend, that it is okay to let it out in a way that honors the Lord. Your venting must not contain any foul language or hateful speech or cause physical harm to another. When you vent, open your heart to the Lord and surrender to Him. Let the Holy Spirit guild you and convict you through it all.

You and I were made to have a daily, personal, and utterly fulfilling relationship with the Lord. We were not made to be separated from Him, yet our sin separates us from Him (Isaiah 59:2). Jesus said in Matthew 11:28-30, "Come to me, all you who are weary and burdened, and I will give you rest. Take my yoke upon you and learn from me, for I am gentle and humble in heart, and you will find rest for your souls. For my yoke is easy, and my burden is light." Go to the Lord when you feel stressed or worried or anxious because He has promised rest to all who are weary. Tell Him how you feel and why you feel that way because He is our High Priest (Hebrews 4), and He has walked this life. He knows and understands.

David's life was filled with ups and downs, and he had to wait 15 years to become King after being anointed. He had to go through many trials, and death was always at his doorstep, yet he trusted the Lord with everything in him. He chose to glorify God and praise Him through all of life's seasons. The Psalms that he wrote are filled with vents and laments. His whole life was laid bare for us to see. David vented to the Lord through all his troubles and also when he sinned. He cried for forgiveness and healing.

Another such example can be seen in the book of Lamentations, where the author is wailing and lamenting over the destruction of Jerusalem. Although this book is filled with vents and frustrations, the author constantly reiterates to the readers' God's faithfulness and goodness. Lamentations 3:22-23 says, "The steadfast love of the Lord never ceases; his mercies never come to an end; they are new every morning; great is your faithfulness." Even through all the pain and destruction, the author kept glorifying God through his venting.

Complaining is a show of dissatisfaction and is usually rooted in deep bitterness. Paul says in Philippians 2:14-15, "Do all things without grumbling or disputing, that you may be blameless and innocent, children of God without blemish in the midst of a crooked and twisted generation, among whom you shine as lights in the world." The point to note here is that we are called to do *'all things'* without complaining and grumbling. We live in a world where complaining is a part of our daily lives. People are dissatisfied with their jobs or spouses or, in general, with the lives they lead. But you know what? God said He would supply *all* our needs (Philippians 4:19), and we know that God is absolutely faithful and His word never fails. He knows our needs, and He is our Shepherd, which means he will take care of everything when we surrender entirely to Him. Why then should we complain? What is our excuse? What is the root of dissatisfaction in our lives? I would request you to take a moment to examine yourself. Ask the Lord to check you and reveal the source of your pain so that you can go to Him in all humility and ask Him to be your provider and corrector.

Adam and Eve were perfect before the fall. They trusted God completely and were fully satisfied in Him. When the devil tempted Eve, he deceived her into thinking she was missing out on something by not eating the fruit of the tree of knowledge of good and evil. The devil tries to convince them that the Lord's plan for their lives is restrictive and oppressive, and he succeeds in doing so. Adam complained to God and blamed Eve, who in turn blamed the serpent. Do you see how the root of complaining is exposed here? It lies in dissatisfaction and the fear of missing out, which is absolutely false because we have everything we will ever need in Christ Jesus. Even in this day and hour, the devil dangles the glory and riches of this world in front of God's children and tries to tempt us into complaining or being dissatisfied with God's plans over our lives.

As children of God, we are the light of the world (Matthew 5:14), and as the verse goes, we cannot be hidden. Our lives are testimonies of God's salvation; as living testimonies, we might be the only reflection of Christ that people may see. So, living in the light of this salvation is crucial, knowing that God's light in us cannot and should not be hidden. Constant grumbling or complaining shows a deep dissatisfaction in God's character and His plans for our lives and isn't really edifying to the soul. I know that life gets hard at times, and I've had days where I was clinging to God by just a thread, but let me assure you that He is faithful. The Lord reminds me of this verse in 2 Timothy 2:14 when I'm weary, and it says, "If we are faithless, he remains faithful, for he cannot disown himself." Know that God is faithful through it all, and He will not leave you because you are His child.

You are found and heard in Christ:

I am going to stop you here and tell you that it is alright to be unhappy in God's presence. Don't get me wrong here, though; there is a fine line between trusting God in our venting versus dishonoring Him through our complaining. Our trials can get a bit too heavy at times, and the pain and sorrow need to come out; they need an escape vent. Many Christians do not know how to talk to God about their problems. We do not know how to express our pain or grief to Him. But, do you know that the Bible encourages the Lord's children to come to Him with their pain?

THE TOXICITY OF CHRONIC COMPLAINING

I want to keep reminding you that you are not alone, dear friend. God is with you every moment of every day. During times of distress, when my soul feels lowly, God reminds me that my walls are continually before Him and that He has engraved my name on the palm of His hands (Isaiah 49:16). Oh, how lovely He is! God knows the deepest depths of your heart. He sees your anxious soul. Your walls are truly ever before Him. Most of us find it difficult to express our emotions, especially the hard ones. We're often mistaken when we believe we can only express gratitude, happy songs, or praise. Do you know that a lot of the Bible is filled with songs of lament and frustration?

God is not afraid to find you in your brokenness. In fact, He is very near to the brokenhearted and saves those who are crushed in spirit (Psalms 34:18). He is not afraid to answer your most painful questions. Every time I feel disheartened and low, I am reminded of Hannah. Hannah had been barren for a long while, and she was deeply distressed because of this. She cried out to the Lord for years, asking Him to open her womb. The word 'Hannah' means favor and grace, which didn't really describe her life at the moment. She was disheartened and in deep anguish.

Every year, Hannah, her husband- Elkanah, and his other wife- Peninnah, went to Shiloh to worship God. One such day, she goes to the Lord's house at Shiloh and starts praying and crying out to Him. Her anguish was clearly visible, and the priest Eli thought that she was drunk, but she told him that she was just pouring out her soul to the Lord (1 Samuel 1:15). Soon after, Hannah gave birth to a baby boy named him Samuel. Now, we all know how mighty a prophet Samuel had been and how the Lord blessed him. You see, Hannah cried out to God for years and years in her barrenness. Her husband's other wife taunted her for years, yet she never gave up and kept praying to the Lord. Hannah wasn't afraid of lamenting and expressing her pain to God. Even in her distress, she honored God when she made a vow to Him, saying, "O Lord of hosts, if you will indeed look on the affliction of your servant and remember me and not forget your servant, but will give to your servant a son, then I will give him to the Lord all the days of his life, and no razor shall touch his head." She honored Him with her prayer, humility, faith, and praise even in her most vulnerable moments. She vented and lamented in her pain but chose to glorify God even in her venting. Dear friend, you are found and heard in Christ. You can always talk to Him about your problems. Do not ignore the pain or suppress it; instead, go to His throne of grace and tell Him your struggles.

The Toll of Chronic Complaining:

Do you know that complaining negatively rewires your brain? Scientists at Stanford University found out that chronic complaining stimulates a permanent change in the structure of the brain's hippocampal region. The Hippocampus is the seat of memory and problem solving, and either constantly complaining or listening to someone complain all the time reduces the size of this region of the brain. Complaining becomes chronic over time because your brain gets used to it, and it's a behavior. Like a sugar or junk food addiction, your brain starts to develop this chronic habit with more exposure.

The more you complain, the more you entertain negative thoughts. Negativity breeds more negativity, and this becomes a vicious cycle over time, and before you know it, this becomes your 'normal.' As complaining shrinks the Hippocampus, it declines your memory and also directly attacks your ability to adapt to new situations. The hormone responsible for stress is called Cortisol, and complaining stimulates the production of this hormone. High levels of cortisol chronically can lead to an array of health problems like high blood pressure, high cholesterol, obesity, increased risk of heart disease and depression, digestive problems, and sleep issues.

Do you know that Optimists tend to live longer lives? Research suggests that optimists are at a 55% lower risk of dying from 11 and a 23% lower risk of dying from heart failure than pessimists. Chronic complaining destroys relationships and affects one's mental health. As Christians, we have every right to go to God and tell Him our problems. Our High Priest (Hebrews 4:14) understands that our lives are fragile and calls us to cry out to Him. Several Biblical characters like Miriam- the sister of Moses, Korah, and Dathan, were subjected to God's anger when they complained against Him (Numbers 12, 16). Chronic complaining that dishonors God and undermines His sovereignty is toxic and can destroy our relationship with the Almighty. Complaining gives the devil a foothold (Ephesians 4:27).

Instead of complaining, appeal to EL ROI, *the God who sees*; for He knows. Hagar called out to EL ROI during her time of distress when she was driven into the wilderness by Sarah. As a result, her needs were met, for she received comfort from the Lord and testified to this saying, "You are the God who sees me (Genesis 16:13)."

Begin to take control:

Taking control starts with surrendering to God completely. I know this seems like a paradox, but our God is a God of the impossible. Begin here. Begin now. Surrender starts by trusting God with His will for our lives, and let me tell you that God's will isn't a bed of roses. We are called to be children of the Most High God, which means He will cleanse and sanctify us to bring us closer and closer to Him. We must learn to listen to His voice rather than to the voice of our selfishness and dissatisfaction.

1. **Become Aware:** Start by becoming actively aware of your thoughts. Ask yourself a few questions and find an accountability partner as it helps to stay focused. Have your thoughts been negative of late? Have you been trusting God and relying on His promises? Have you been grumbling about things? Start maintaining a mental health journal where you can write down how you feel and why you've been feeling that way. Go to the root of the problem. Be keen to notice repetitive patterns and address them.
2. **Repent of Complaining:** If you notice that you've been complaining and grumbling a lot of late, go to God and repent. Ask God to convict you of this; this is where you surrender. Nothing compares to having the gift of salvation and being a child of the Most High God. Dwell in this and remind yourself of God's goodness whenever you feel like complaining. His grace is never too far, and know that He will forgive you if you go to Him. Don't run away from Him in times of trouble; instead, run to Him (Psalm 50:15).
3. **Shift your thoughts and conversations:** God says in Jeremiah 29:11, "For I know the plans I have for you," declares the Lord, "plans to prosper you and not to harm you, plans to give you hope and a future." God's promise for ALL His children. He has good plans for you. The creator of all things loves and cherishes you. Isn't this a reason to be extra joyful? I cannot stop jumping and dancing when I think of this. I just get so excited! When negativity seems to creep in, fight it with God's promises.

4. **Have compassion for yourself**: Learn to have compassion for yourself, especially when things go wrong or when you falter. Being critical of yourself isn't the solution. Instead, count your blessings and trust that God will see you through this.
5. **Respond in Faith and practice Gratitude:** Respond to complaining or negativity with prayer. Pray your way through life's most challenging situations, and embrace lamenting. God is with you (Isaiah 41:10), and He is for you (Romans 8:31). He is the same God who gave up His very own begotten Son to save you from sin. Oh, how He loves you! Maintain a gratitude journal where you can write down everything you're grateful for. You can also write down all the promises of God that have come to be.

2

YOUR THOUGHT LIFE

"For as he thinks in his heart, so is he."

— -PROVERBS 23:7

*E*mma and Jenny entered my life when I needed the sweetness of friendship. They were my sisters in Christ. We loved talking about everything in life, from Jesus Christ to our daily struggles to our darkest fears. Jenny was the most intelligent person you'd ever meet, shockingly straightforward and sharp as cheddar. She was filled with love and empathy towards those around her. She was a giver and always supported and encouraged people. On the other hand, Emma was the sweetest thing, she loved life, and everyone around her admired her. She was pleasant, kind, and gentle like a soft rose. She was always polite and compassionate to those around her.

These two were very dear to my heart; I love them. The three of us walked through the many seasons of life together.

You see, Emma and Jenny were like sugar and spice; they were completely different people, and the way they reacted to situations was quite the opposite. Jenny was an eternal optimist and someone who saw the best in every case. She was a fighter. The thing that inspired me the most was that Jenny prayed her way through life, and trust me, her life was not easy. She had a harrowing childhood, and up to this day, her relationship with her parents is rocky.

On the other hand, Emma was quite soft-hearted and emotional. This lady was a rock who supported Jenny and me through all our ups and downs. I love Emma's nature because she was always present and helpful in times of need. The one thing about Emma was that she was a chronic complainer. Being an emotional person, she felt life on a deeper level and absorbed emotions like a sponge. We'd hear how bad her day was or how a particular person had hurt her. She'd complain about her marriage, her in-laws, or her health. Jenny and I tried to jump in and help her because we cared for her, but she started spiraling into her mind more often. Her constant complaining started impacting her daily life; she started having mild anxiety attacks. The smallest of things started bothering her, and she found it hard to let things go. Her life was a reflection of her thoughts. As she let the negativity in, it became her definition of 'normal.' Our dear Emma suffered from anxiety for years. Still, the good news is that she finally managed to take control of the situation. But you see how Emma's thoughts were transformed into powerful emotions that then took hold of her and changed her entire life?

Freedom starts with surrender. Emma's liberation started the day she decided that God was the answer. But we all know that our actions have to match our thoughts. Convincing your mind isn't enough unless your actions start to align with your mind. Are you feeling trapped? Do you think life is going on and you're just stuck there? Does the anxiety feel overwhelming at times? Have your thoughts been ruling your life off late? Let me tell you that you can win this war! Life doesn't have to be this way. Do you know what Solomon wrote of life in the book of Ecclesiastes? Let us look at Ecclesiastes 11:9-10, which says:

> *"You who are young, be happy while you are young, and let your heart give you joy in the days of your youth. Follow the ways of your heart and whatever your eyes see, but know that for all these things, God will bring you into judgment. So then, banish anxiety from your heart and cast off the troubles of your body, for youth and vigor are meaningless."*
>
> — ECCLESIASTES 11:9-10

Life is a gift of God. As the verse goes, we are called to banish anxiety from our hearts. Anxiety drains us of our joy and happiness, but these exact things are a gift of God. We must take every opportunity to enjoy this gift of life under the light of God's salvation. We must do this knowing that God will judge us for everything and that we are accountable for every second of our lives. When you receive a gift from someone, do you throw it away? Certainly not! You open it with excitement and savor the gift because it has been given out of love. You're reminded of how much the giver loves you every time you look at it.

In the same way, is it good for us to throw away God's gift of life? Your Creator knows what you've been through in life. You are in His loving care. In His sovereignty, the Lord says in Isaiah 30:15, "In repentance and rest is your salvation, in quietness and trust is your strength." He knows what your future holds; He holds your future. In all of life's uncertainties, He holds you. Through every season of life, God walks with us. He has given us (His children) the joy of His salvation and a peace that surpasses all understanding (Romans 15:13). How do we live in His victory? Let us dig a little deeper to understand the root of complaining.

What are thoughts?

I love reading the book of Psalms. It contains songs of deep emotion and vulnerability. It strips all emotional coverings and shows the bare human heart. In one of my favorite Psalms, the Psalmist sings a song of intimacy and love when he says, "For you created my inmost being; you knit me together in my mother's womb. I praise you because I am fearfully and wonderfully made; your works are wonderful, I know that full well (Psalm 139:13-14)." The verse cuts through my soul every single time I read it. The Creator of the universe, the One who made the sky and suspended the stars in absolute nothingness, knit you together in your mother's womb. He made you to be fearful and wonderful. Dear friend, you are lovely and were created to be this wonderful person. Isn't this a beautiful gift? God knows the deepest parts of your heart. There is nothing hidden from Him (Hebrews 4:13). This is your identity: You are His child, and you are fearfully and wonderfully made.

We live in a fallen and sin-cursed world where sin is everywhere. We are all born in sin (Psalm 51:5). No one is sinless (Romans 3:23). Sin has tainted our world, and the only light in this world is Jesus Christ. King Solomon said in Ecclesiastes 1:13, "It is an unhappy business that God has given to the children of man to be busy with." This is the reality of life according to the Bible. The curse of sin is upon all humankind, and this harsh reality is a consequence of it. The thoughts we have are fallen too. Now coming to the topic of discussion, what are thoughts? Thoughts are the mental ideas, beliefs, and opinions we form throughout life. They determine the quality of lives we will lead. For example, your attitude is created by multiple situations you have been exposed to over time. It directly results from your perception of things, family beliefs, childhood outcomes, and genetics.

The flesh, which is just a tent that we live in (2 Corinthians 5:1), has a significant impact on our thoughts, and so does the external world. Does this mean that we cannot control our thoughts? Are negative thoughts inevitable? The answer to these questions is no and yes. Our mind is conscious and aware of the thoughts it processes and the actions it takes. Therefore, we can control our thoughts. But on the other hand, negative thoughts are inevitable, partly because of our fallen nature and separation from God. This does not justify dwelling on the negative thoughts until they start to take over. It is possible to take control of your thoughts and steer clear of negativity. Research suggests that your genetics determine 50% of your happiness, your circumstances determine 10%, and the remaining 40% is based on your effort to stay happy. You don't have to succumb to the lies of the devil. The Bible says in John 17:17, "Sanctify them by the truth; your word is truth." The truth of the Word ALWAYS defeats the lies of the devil.

But why do our thoughts directly affect the quality of our lives? You see, our thoughts are transformed into emotions, usually expressed as actions. The joy, anger, hurt, or happiness you feel are products of either external actions or internal thoughts. Before you react to any situation, your brain has to process the stimulus or the thought. The brain processes it based on preconceived notions or past experiences. To understand this, let us look at the Pharisees and Sadducees, who were both figures of authority during Biblical times. They were men of high intellectual understanding and great learning. They viewed the world through their high standards of tradition. Anything that did not fit their definition of righteousness was rejected. They rejected Jesus Christ because He didn't fit their notion of the Messiah. Do you see how their thoughts deceived them? Their thoughts were translated into emotions, and this can be seen by their pure hatred for Christ (Mark 3:6). Their thoughts and actions became detrimental to such a degree that they plotted the murder of Christ and succeeded in doing so. Do you see how their thoughts condemned them? Harmful thoughts can destroy us if we entertain them.

Uncovering the invisible enemy:

Your thoughts will make or break you. What you entertain is what you will become. Do you see how your negative thoughts are the invisible enemy? Beliefs aren't formed in a day; they are created by layers of thoughts that the mind has promoted. Did you know that about 40 million adults in the U.S. are slaves to depression and anxiety? This accounts for about 20% of the country's population. You do not have to be a slave to your negative thinking. This invisible enemy does not have to be a stronghold in your life. I understand this may have become a way of life for many of us because we've been clinging to our negative thinking patterns for years. But don't let this stronghold deter you because God is still on the throne.

Romans 8:28 says, "And we know that in all things God works for the good of those who love him, who have been called according to his purpose." My favorite part of this verse is that ALL THINGS work for good because we are His children. Let me remind you that our heavenly Father isn't like humans. Human beings change according to the season, but He is constant. He is the same forever and ever. The Lord says in Isaiah 49:15, "Can a mother forget the baby at her breast and have no compassion on the child she has borne? Though she may forget, I will not forget you!" He won't leave you with your thoughts. Suffering from negative thinking for years and feeling that all hope is lost, hold onto this promise now! Your Father will not leave you, and all things will work for good for you. God has defeated the enemy. Our God is a God of the impossible. Have faith in Him because He is more than able.

Let me walk you through the story of Gideon in the Bible. During the days of the Judges, the Israelites were being oppressed by the Midianites; they cried out to God. In response to this, the Lord sends an angel to a man named Gideon and calls out, saying, "The Lord is with you, O mighty man of valor." You see, God viewed Gideon as a man of courage because this was a gift of God to Gideon. The angel of the Lord told Gideon that he would rescue the Israelites from the hand of the Midianites. But Gideon started complaining to God and doubting Him. Finally, he replied to the angel, saying that his clan was the weakest in the tribe of Manasseh and that he was the least in his father's house. Do you see how Gideon's thinking condemned him even though the Lord affirmed Him and showed him his true identity? He was so used to dwelling on his negative thinking and being defeated by it that he did not even heed the word of the Lord here. As the story goes on, Gideon tested God not once but thrice because of his doubt and defeated thinking. But you know what? Praise God for His goodness and patience because Gideon went on to win the war through impossible situations. But the key takeaway here is that Gideon's thinking was his enemy. A lot of times, we find ourselves stuck in the same place as Gideon. Our thoughts condemn us, and we choose disbelief. We choose our negative thinking and start to complain.

Do you want to end up in a spiral of negativity, dear friend? Or do you want to change like Gideon and conquer your thought life? Your bad past does not have to define your future. Your current circumstances do not have to dictate your future. Let me talk about faith for a while here. Do you know that faith comes from hearing God's word (Romans 10:17)? When a Christian is lost in her (or his) negative thinking, she is undermining the character of God. It shows a lack of faith because you choose to trust your situation rather than God's plan and will. Take a few moments to ask the Holy Spirit to convict you of your faith, dear friend. This is between you and the Lord, and when you ask, He is faithful to give. Ask Him where it went wrong and repent if this is you. It is impossible to please the Lord without faith (Hebrews 11:6). The apostles asked Jesus to increase their faith in Luke 17, Jesus replied, "If you have faith as small as a mustard seed, you can say to this mulberry tree, 'Be uprooted and planted in the sea,' and it will obey you." Ask the Lord to give you the faith of a mustard seed, dear friend.

King Solomon said in Proverbs 4:23, "Be careful what you think because your thoughts run your life." We know Solomon was the wisest man and knew that our thoughts, not our circumstances, run our lives. Now that you've spent time with the Lord, asking Him to reveal these things to you, let me talk about how the shifting of our thinking from the negative side to a more faith-filled positive side glorifies God. Once you're saved and born again into the kingdom of God, you become a daughter of Yahweh. You are adopted into His family. Paul wrote in 1 Corinthians 1:18, "For the word of the cross is folly to those who are perishing, but to us who are being saved it is the power of God." The tense used by Paul here is *'being saved.'* As believers, our salvation is threefold: we are first saved when we receive Jesus Christ as our Lord (Ephesians 2:8-9), and this is the process of *justification*. We are being saved in the present and will continue to be saved until the day we die (1 Corinthians 1:18), and this is the process of *sanctification*. One day, Jesus will save us entirely by finishing His sanctifying work in us (Philippians

1:6), and this is called *glorification*. As believers, we are being sanctified daily by God.

If you think you've been quite the complainer, do not worry, for God will help you deal with it. It is all a part of His process of sanctifying us. The Holy Spirit is our helper (John 15:26) and guide. The Bible says in Romans 8:26-27, "Likewise the Spirit also helps in our weaknesses. For we do not know what we should pray for as we ought, but the Spirit Himself makes intercession for us with groanings which cannot be uttered. Now He who searches the hearts knows what the mind of the Spirit *is* because He makes intercession for the saints according to *the will of* God." Paul clearly states that the Holy Spirit helps us in our weaknesses, mainly when we cannot express or even talk to God about it. The second part of the verse talks about how the Holy Spirit intercedes for the saints (us) according to God's will, and let me tell you that God's will for us is sanctification. He is purifying us by the day and bringing us closer to the image of Christ, which also applies to our negative thinking. Let me tell you that this doesn't happen overnight, and you will not wake up tomorrow feeling 100% Optimistic, but it is a process. The process of cleaning our minds will not be easy. It will be painful and hard but know that God's ways are higher and better than ours. He will progressively and gradually bring you out of your negativity and move you into greener pastures of His promises, where your thoughts will be positive and healthy. Now, this does not mean we can sit in our negative minds and give up on being more positive. On the contrary, we must make every effort to change our thoughts and stop complaining.

How to fight the invisible war?

You cannot defeat that which you cannot define. If you do not diagnose the disease, you cannot treat it. In the same way, if you do not understand your patterns, you cannot address them. You have to start by taking your thoughts captive.' Pay close attention to what you think and the patterns you're used to having. Take responsibility for your thoughts and patterns here. In an age where mental illness is rampant, taking care of yourself and your thoughts is mandatory. What does the Bible have to say about this invisible war? The Apostle Paul wrote in Ephesians 6:12, "For we do not wrestle against flesh and blood, but the rulers, against the authorities, against the cosmic powers over this present darkness, against the spiritual forces of evil in the heavenly places." Fighting against these powers in the heavenly realm seems a bit scary, doesn't it? Let me remind you that God is for us and the Holy Spirit dwells in us (1 Corinthians 3:16). How do we win this invisible war?

Paul answered this question in 2 Corinthians 10:3-5, where he said, "For though we walk in the flesh, we are not waging war according to the flesh. For the weapons of our warfare are not of the flesh but have divine power to destroy strongholds. We destroy arguments and every lofty opinion raised against the knowledge of God, and take every thought captive to obey Christ." The verse states that although we are flesh (human), our weapons are divine. I shall go into detail about this in the next few chapters, but this is the power that has been given to us. Now, in our case, these 'strongholds' are negative thinking and complaining. The second half of the above verse talks about 'taking every thought captive to obey Christ.' This means we should take our thoughts captive and submit to Christ by bringing them under control. We are called to glorify God in everything we do (1 Corinthians 10:31), which means we are called to glorify Him even with our thoughts. How do we do this? How do we control these thoughts and submit them to Christ when our mind fires away in a million directions?

There is a way to do this. You see, the Christian life is

fantastic. I have seen God change the impossible. He doesn't just make it better; He makes it spectacular! God will make a way. The next chapter will discuss the various principles we can implement to win this war against our minds. In retrospection, have you been listening to the conviction of the Holy Spirit? Have you repented of your sin? Have you softened your heart to His word?

3

THE PATTERNS THAT KEEP YOU STUCK

"Be careful what you think because your thoughts run your life."

— PROVERBS 4:23

Do you know who you are? But, more importantly, do you know who you are in Christ Jesus? What is your identity in Him? After I received the gift of salvation, I realized that everything changed for me: I was no longer the person I once was; I am a child of God. As my Father's daughter, my identity lies in Christ alone. I am not defined by my circumstances, family problems, financial status, or anything else that once described me. I am not inferior. You see, I always struggled with my self-esteem because of my past. I was a captive to my thoughts; my thoughts ran my life and dictated my future. But you know what? God freed me the day He gave me a revelation about Himself.

The Bible says in Isaiah 61:1-3,

SIS, COMPLAINING IS REMAINING IN TOXIC THINKING

> *"The Spirit of the Sovereign Lord is on me because the Lord has anointed me to proclaim good news to the poor. He has sent me to bind up the brokenhearted, to proclaim freedom for the captives and release from darkness for the prisoners, to proclaim the year of the Lord's favor and the day of vengeance of our God, to comfort all who mourn, and provide for those who grieve in Zion— to bestow on them a crown of beauty instead of ashes, the oil of joy instead of mourning, and a garment of praise instead of a spirit of despair."*
>
> — ISAIAH 61:1-3

This verse changed my entire life! I pray that the Lord makes His light shine on His Word so that you may see it in power and truth. Jesus came to free the captives. He came to bind your broken heart. He came to comfort you in your mourning. Do you know what he gives instead of the ashes of our life? He provides us with a crown of beauty, the oil of joy, and a garment of praise. I was once captive to my thoughts, but now I'm free in Him. He not only freed me but gave me beauty and joy instead of the pain I once felt. Now I live to praise and glorify Him for all the days of my life. You don't have to be captive to your thoughts, dear friend. Come to the throne of grace and exchange this brokenness for beauty. Come to the altar.

Every time life gets heavy, and the negativity starts creeping in, remember that Jesus came to free you. I stumbled across something that A. W. Tozer once said, "When the Lord lays His hand upon a man, that man ceases at once to be ordinary. He immediately becomes extraordinary, and his life takes on cosmic significance. The angels in heaven take notice of him and go forth to become his ministers (Hebrews 1:14). Though the man had before been only one of the faceless multitudes, a mere cipher in the universe. A man was an invisible dust grain blown across endless wastes–now he gets a face and a name and a place in the scheme of meaningful things. Christ knows His own sheep 'by name.' There are no unknown Christians, no insignificant sons of God. Each one signifies each is a "sign" drawing the attention of the Triune God Day and night upon him. The faceless man has a face, the nameless man a name when Jesus picks him out of the multitude and calls him to Himself." Our God knows us by name. He would've died for you on the cross even if you were the only one on the earth. Oh, what love has been bestowed upon us! When God looks at us, He views us through the image of Christ. His righteousness has been placed upon us (Isaiah 61:10). Your thoughts don't define you; Jesus does.

Cultivating Self-Awareness:

Now that we've seen who we truly are in Christ, I want to ask you one more question. Do you confront your negative thoughts, or do you push them aside and pretend that they never occurred? Many of us are guilty of doing this. Sweeping something under the rug is not necessarily getting rid of it; it is just a temporary solution to mask it. Ignoring your emotions or bottling them up is very unhealthy. Repressed emotions cause a great deal of physical stress. A study conducted by Harvard University found out that bottling your emotions can increase your chances of premature death by 30%, and the risk of being diagnosed with cancer increases by a whopping 70%.

Hiding your negative thoughts will not remove them. You must take responsibility and confront them. Being aware of our thoughts and who we are is quite important. You have to face the reality of your thoughts and emotions. As Christians, we are called to deny ourselves, carry our crosses, and follow Christ (Matthew 16:24-26). Denying yourself doesn't mean ignoring the potentially toxic thoughts that could pile up over time and ruin your life. This is where we need to exercise wisdom and understand the difference between following God's Word and using it as an excuse to avoid dealing with the situation. Being aware of yourself and your identity in Christ is the same. You are a new creation in Christ Jesus (2 Corinthians 5:17). You are who He says you are. You are found in Him.

Naomi lived with her family in the land of Moab when a great famine broke out. She then lost both her sons right after the death of her husband, Elimelek. She was utterly broken. She was now survived by two of her widowed daughters-in-law, Ruth and Orpah. After a while, she heard the Lord had provided food for His people of Judah, and they decided to return to Bethlehem. Naomi was in great pain and wasn't afraid to express it. Before the journey, she urged her daughters-in-law to return to their own homes and said in Ruth 1:13, "No, my daughters. It is more bitter for me than for you because the Lord's hand has turned against me!" She didn't evade her emotions. She knew the reality of her situation and wasn't afraid to voice her lament. Finally, one of her daughters-in-law, Orpah, went home to her family, but Ruth chose to follow Naomi to Bethlehem.

As they reach the city of Bethlehem, the women recognize Naomi and start talking to her. To this, Naomi replies, "Don't call me Naomi. Call me Mara because the Almighty has made my life very bitter. I went away full, but the Lord has brought me back empty. Why call me Naomi? The Lord has afflicted me; the Almighty has brought misfortune upon me (Ruth 1:20-21)." She didn't deny her circumstance and brought her lament to God. As the story continues, we know that the Lord showed up most amazingly, and Naomi's cry was heard. Her daughter-in-law, Ruth, married Boaz and had a son Obed. Out of Obed's line came David, and we all know that Jesus was of the line of David.

Self-awareness is important. Knowing where you are and choosing to voice your pain to God isn't wrong. God wants us to go to Him just like Naomi did. You don't have to deny your pain or negativity and hide behind it. Life isn't always sunshine and roses, and the frailties of this life are many. Being aware of yourself is not a sin. Taking care of your mind is not a sin. Be honest with God and yourself. The Bible says in 2 Corinthians 13:5, "Examine yourselves, whether ye be in the faith; prove your own selves. Know ye, not your own selves, how that Jesus Christ is in you, except ye be reprobates?" Unless you know what your soul holds and what is happening inside you, you cannot be disciplined in the faith.

Thought patterns:

Did you know that your thought patterns define your perception of reality? Most negative thinking patterns are unrealistic and stem from either past or present fears. The worst outcome of these thoughts is that they have massive impacts on our emotions, and emotions usually translate into actions. The science behind negative patterns of thinking is quite simple: negativity breeds more and more negativity. Our brains are hardwired to recall negative experiences over positive ones, and we know that our memories or past experiences dictate how we perceive the world around us. Research conducted by Harvard University found that a single negative setback has double the effect on our memory compared to a positive experience. Your brain processes situations that involve stress in great detail. These situations are stored in your long-term memory, and your brain dwells on them for future reference. This is how thought patterns are formed.

Did you know that ruminating on negative thoughts creates an endless self-defeating cycle that decelerates your body's healing process? One painful situation is enough to begin a cyclic pattern of negativity. Our thoughts can indeed dictate our life. Our thoughts turn into feelings which then get translated into actions. Finally, the actions we take will define our life. A small spring of negative thoughts gets translated into an endless cycle of unhappy actions. If a person says they haven't had any negative thoughts in their life, they are lying. The frailty of this fallen world, we are exposed to the fallen nature, which is subjected to negativity and sin.

If you've been stuck in these negative thought patterns, you're not alone. These destructive patterns can be changed. The Bible says in John 8:32, "Then you will know the truth, and the truth will set you free." Knowing the truth and actively applying it to your life is the answer to this problem. You can release yourself from these negative patterns by constructively aligning yourself with the word of God. Most of us just pray over our negative patterns thinking that the Lord will change everything. Of course, the Lord is more than capable of changing everything for you, but we often forget that we have to cooperate with Him as well.

Daniel was known as one who was highly esteemed by the Lord (Daniel 10:19). During the reign of King Cyrus of Persia, Daniel received a revelation through a vision. He didn't quite know what it meant and sought to understand its meaning, so he fasted and prayed for three weeks. During these three weeks, he reframed from food (meat or wine) and entirely devoted himself to praying and seeking answers. We then see that his prayer was answered when the Lord sent a messenger to reveal the true meaning of the vision to Daniel. Did you see how Daniel carried out his role by praying and fasting? The Lord answered Daniel's prayer because He was desperate and aligned himself with God's will. Daniel was desperate, and he made sure his actions followed his prayers.

God doesn't need our help to make things happen, but He

wants us to work with Him and build a deeper relationship with Him. This is why we have to cooperate with our God. Start by recognizing your need for Him. Then, you must accept that your thought patterns need to be changed. Prayer indeed is how we fight the war, but you must also play your part.

Identifying your thought patterns:

How are we supposed to identify our negative thought patterns? To answer the question, let us perform a small exercise. I want you to take a piece of paper to write down the questions mentioned below. You can even use a journal if you find it more comfortable. Write down these questions and give yourself to answer them:

- Do I consider myself a failure?
- How often do my thoughts wander away?
- Do I wake up feeling grateful every morning, or do I wake up feeling moody and sad?
- How often do I think about preventing my past failures?
- Do I dwell on or think about my childhood mistakes often?
- Do I keep questioning every decision I make?
- What are the other negative experiences that haunt my mind?
- What are the main experiences that come to mind whenever I feel low or scared?

Once you answer these questions, I want you to think about your relationship with God and answer the following questions:

- Do I trust the Lord with all my sins and failures?

SIS, COMPLAINING IS REMAINING IN TOXIC THINKING

- How is my current relationship with God? (Answer in detail; be honest with yourself here).
- Have I surrendered all aspects of my life to God?
- Do I make it a point to pray about God's will and live in it?
- What promises of God do I stand on during times of adversity?
- Have I been praying and exercising my faith?

Where do you think you stand after answering all these questions? I hope that you've started to understand your areas of weakness. It is crucial not just to understand your flaws but to take action to deal with them. Because of our fallen nature, our thoughts can be influenced by the world or the flesh. The spirit and flesh are constantly at war, and the flesh desires that which is contrary to the spirit (Galatians 5:17). But the good news is that God has not given us a spirit of fear but of power, love, and a sound mind (2 Timothy 1:7). We can control our minds because God has already given us the weapons of warfare.

Sometimes, I hear myself saying, 'I have no control over my life; I feel helpless when I get overwhelmed with frustration with my circumstances. But then I remember what God says in Isaiah 41:10, "Fear not, for I am with you; be not dismayed, for I am your God; I will strengthen you, I will help you, I will uphold you with my righteous right hand." God is always with me as He is always with you. You are His child, and He never leaves His children to fend for themselves. So even if you feel helpless, He is in control and knows what you're facing.

When I feel that sickness is going to attack, I subconsciously promote this negative thought, but what are we supposed to do when such thoughts enter our minds? The Bible says in Isaiah 53:5, "He was pierced for our transgressions; he was crushed for our iniquities; upon him was the chastisement that brought us peace, and with his wounds, we are healed." So I am supposed to condemn the negative thought or the sickness with the word of God. I am to speak it out and declare it over my body, not just think it in my mind.

Some of us have been beaten down and bruised for a long time, and as a result, we feel utterly hopeless. I remember facing a fiery trial for more than six months. It left me wholly exhausted and drained out, and because of this, I kept telling myself that nothing good would ever happen to me. But God says in Jeremiah 29:11, "For I know the plans I have for you, plans to prosper you and not to harm you, plans to give you hope and a future." When God has promised this to me, how can I not cling to this hope? I know that trusting God above our circumstances is challenging. But we know that it is only through faith that we can please Him (Hebrews 11:6).

Another thought that is a frequent visitor is 'I am not good enough.' It comes in many forms like 'I'm not nice enough,' 'I am not good enough for my husband,' 'I am not enough for my children,' 'I am not a good Christian, and God won't use me.' 'I am not good enough because I've been a failure in life.' These are just a handful of the many self-condemning thoughts that haunt me as a person. I'm sure a lot of us encounter such thoughts often. The truth is we are not good enough according to the righteous standards of God. But the good news is that we are found in Jesus Christ. Our identity lies in Him; through Him, we are good enough. His righteousness has been imparted on us (2 Corinthians 5:21). Always remember that you have been fearfully and wonderfully made (Psalm 139:13-14). I shall discuss combating such negative thoughts in further chapters.

We live in the 21st century, and sin is rampant. It is ubiquitous and almost inevitable. With the growing evil, we may ask ourselves how it is that we can control the negativity around us? The Bible answers this question in Romans 5:20, saying, "The law was brought in so that the trespass might increase. But where sin increased, grace increased all the more so that, just as sin reigned in death, so also grace might reign through righteousness to bring eternal life through Jesus Christ our Lord." This verse states that God's abounding grace is more profound no matter how deep sin has snuck in. It penetrates the most negative of minds. So if you think you are lost in your thought patterns, remember that grace abounds deeper than anxiety. God always has the final word. He has lavished His mercy and grace because we are His children. This does not mean we continue to live in our negative thinking; instead, we go to the throne of grace and let His goodness envelop us.

In knowing yourself, you know God:

Working on a godly thought life is challenging but worthwhile. We all have our weaknesses, and I'd be lying if I said I'm perfect. God is glorified in our weaknesses as Paul spoke of the thorn in his flesh (2 Corinthians 12). Now we do not know what the thorn in Paul's flesh was. It could have been a physical, emotional, or spiritual struggle. Paul says that he pleaded with the Lord to take away thrice. 2 Corinthians 12:9 says, "But he said to me, "My grace is sufficient for you, for my power is made perfect in weakness." Therefore I will boast all the more gladly about my weaknesses so that Christ's power may rest on me." This was the Lord's reply to Paul's prayer. Paul said he would boast about his weakness because it displays Christ's power in him. God gives us His grace and strength in our weaknesses.

A.W. Tozer once said, "Make your thoughts a sanctuary God can inhabit, and don't let any of the rest of your life dishonor God." I love how Tozer reminds us to invite God into our thoughts so that He can live there. Jesus is the Prince of peace. Can you imagine the Prince of peace ruling your thought life? I would be overjoyed and dance my way through life, which is my reality. Surrender your thought patterns to Him. He will mold you and keep you in perfect peace. If you think the past has been dictating your present, come to the Healer and the altar of grace. He makes all things new. Isaiah 26:3 says, "You will keep him in perfect peace, whose mind is stayed on You because he trusts in You." Peace is a gift to all of us. Shift your mind to Him, dear friend. Cast all your cares on Him because He cares for you (1 Peter 5:7).

Don't become discouraged if you fall back into an old sin habit or negative thought life. The devil wants to feel defeated and keep you in that pattern of thinking. Don't believe his lies. Don't ever forget that all things are possible with God, and He is more than able to change things. Start taking action and fight every negative thought with God's word. Keep dwelling on His promises and repeat them until you've memorized them. Psalm 119:11 says, "I have hidden your word in my heart that I might not sin against you." His word conquers all evil. Always remember that God is with you and is fighting for you. You just need to participate and do your part. You can break this pattern. Just believe.

4

RENEWAL – CONQUERING NEGATIVE THOUGHT

"Be transformed by the renewing of your mind."

— ROMANS 12:2

*J*oyce Meyer once said, "You cannot have a positive life and a negative mind." We all want to be happy and fulfilled. The question is, are you building a positive life? Are your thoughts proof of that? It's okay if you do not always have positive thoughts because everyone struggles with negative thoughts from time to time. But have you been consistently struggling with these destructive thoughts? Some of us have subjected our minds to negative thoughts for so long that it has become our 'normal.' We can no longer differentiate between a toxic thought and a normal thought. As such, we need to understand the different ways in which these thoughts attack us.

What do negative thoughts sound like?

We will perform a small exercise before getting further

into this chapter. In Chapter 3, you were asked to answer a few questions to identify your thought patterns. I want you to review the answers for a minute here. Were your responses primarily negative? I need you to examine yourself to understand the root of your intentions. How are your thoughts?

To understand your thoughts, I will share a few common types of patterns that most people fall into. Some of us have developed an 'All-or-Nothing' thinking, where we view the world in black and white. You either consider yourself a complete success or an utter failure, and there is no grey area here. As a result, you have seasons of ultra-positive days and then deal with seasons of extreme negativity. Some of us tend to overgeneralize things based on one or two significant incidents. For example, you fail to accomplish a goal once or twice and conclude that you are a failure. This type of thinking leads to a vicious cycle of negativity. Another school of thought is to view the world through a mental filter. For example, your partner says something negative about you, and you start to feel lost. You conclude that the relationship is doomed by choosing to ignore years of positive comments.

Some of us choose to ignore or disqualify the positive. For example, your friend compliments you on looking good, and you just brush it away, thinking that she's just 'being nice.' Even though the experience was positive, you chose to ignore it. A few of us 'mind-read' situations or people and usually jump to conclusions. This type of thinking is generally very judgy and inaccurate. Meeting a new person and instantly concluding that they have certain unlikable traits is something I am guilty of at times when it isn't healthy. Sometimes, we tend to maximize or minimize an experience. Many of us tend to be hard on ourselves for a small mistake or when something we cannot change occurs. We exaggerate the importance of this literally with a pair of binoculars.

A widespread type of reasoning we deal with is called Emotional reasoning. Most of us are guilty of entertaining this type of thinking. We rely on our emotions instead of reality. For example, you feel that your partner isn't spending enough time with you because of a fight, but the truth is that he's been swamped at work late. You hold onto these emotional feelings instead of just looking at the facts. Most of us tend to live in the future instead of the present. We use statements like 'When I finally get…,' or 'Once I've bought…,' or 'I should get skinny by….' These statements or unrealistic expectations push us into feeling guilty often. When we don't meet our expectations, we become disappointed and call ourselves 'failures.' We tirelessly wait for better days when life is happening now.

Sometimes, we end up labeling people out of our judgments. Few of us are guilty of taking things too personally. Instead, we tend to blame ourselves for every small thing that goes wrong. This pattern of behavior can lead to extreme moodiness or irritation. For example, someone decides to skip a dinner party, and you end up taking it very personally. All these types of thoughts or actions become patterns over a while. They become the standard way of dealing with situations.

Conquering negative thoughts:

There are usually two sources of negative thinking, the first being your flesh or the carnal mind and the second being evil or demonic spirits. The earth is covered in darkness (Isaiah 60:2), and the devil is the ruler or god of this world (2 Corinthians 4:4). The Bible talks about a spirit of despair in Isaiah 61:3, where it is prophesied that Jesus comes to give us a garment of praise instead of the spirit of despair (heaviness). These are oppressive spirits that entice us into negative thinking, anxiety, and depression. Some of these evil spirits can be familiar spirits that attack genealogies. They attack regions they're familiar with or families they've previously attacked (Mark 5:9-10).

In his sermon titled *'How to be delivered from demons and demonic oppression,'* Derek Prince describes demons as persons without bodies. He says that we must realize that we are dealing with a person. Demons torment and entice us. But does this excuse us from exercising the word of God? It most certainly does not! In his book, *They shall expel demons: What you need to know about demons- you invisible enemies*, Derek Prince says, "At this point, God taught me another important lesson: He would do for me what I could not do for myself, but He would not do for me what He required me to do for myself. God had responded to my cry and delivered me from the spirit of heaviness, but after that, He held me responsible to exercise scriptural discipline over my thoughts." God will deliver you from your captivity if you cry out to Him, but the rest is up to you. You are entirely responsible for what you think. You cannot constantly live in negativity by entertaining it and blaming God for failing in this area. You will have to exercise a great deal of spiritual discipline.

Christ has already trampled the devil under His foot, and you and I are partakers of this victory. The Bible says in 2 Corinthians 10:5, "Take every thought captive to make it obedient to Christ." We are to bring our thoughts under Christ's captivity because He can. We cannot do this in our strength. Now the question is, how do we do this? A few practical ways to take every thought captive are:

1. **Start by accepting responsibility for your thoughts:** You are responsible for your thoughts. We are usually defiled by that which comes out of

us (Mark 7:20-22). There is always a path in front of you from which you are to choose what you want. Out of the abundance of our hearts, our thoughts are expressed through our mouths (Matthew 12:34). Check your heart, and ask the Holy Spirit to reveal its condition to you. Is your heart pure? Cain was asked to focus on the right, pure, and righteous things by the Lord, but he chose to dwell on his impure and jealous thoughts. We all know how the story turned out with Cain committing the first murder by killing his brother. Start by confessing to the Lord that you are weak and surrender to Him.

2. **Focus on changing the way you think:** You see, God is in the business of redeeming and sanctifying His people. He makes us more like His Son with each passing day (John 3:30). Don't worry if your thoughts have been bad since day one because God wants to heal your mind. He wants to renew your mindset. He is sanctifying His saints. You have to perform your role by disciplining your mind. You must not entertain toxic or intrusive thoughts. When your thoughts get too overwhelming, be still and know that He is God (Psalm 46:10). He will calm the storm within you.

3. **Get up and embrace God's gift of nature:** I've had days where everything gets so heavy, and I desperately need an outlet. This beautiful earth is God's gift to us, which is why he placed it under our stewardship. So when the devil has got you down, get up and go for a run or a walk. Embrace God's gift of nature; welcome the distraction and use it as a healthy outlet. The Bible says in Hebrews 12:1, "Let us throw off everything that

hinders and the sin that so easily entangles. And let us run with perseverance the race marked out for us." We are called to persevere because God is 100% faithful. Heaven will meet your every need, your every need, child of God.
4. **Sweet surrender:** To take captive every thought and make it obedient to Christ, you must confess and surrender. The battle always belongs to the Lord. I remember fighting battles where I just couldn't do it anymore. Life gets so exhausting at times, and our minds are fragile. Just surrender to God; He will fight the battle. David was able to defeat the giant Goliath with a stone and a sling. Gideon and his army of merely 300 men could defeat 135,000 enemy soldiers. You don't have to fight the battle; surrender to God.
5. **Memorize the word of God:** When God gives you a promise or a revelation, memorize it. God has given His children His armor which is shown in Ephesians 6. Use the helmet of salvation to protect your head from the enemy's attacks and the sword of the Spirit, which is the word of God to slay the enemy (Ephesians 6:17). I'll go deep into these weapons of warfare in further chapters. When you feel that the enemy is attacking you, speak out the word of God; don't just think it but speak it out loud.
6. **Change your focus:** We know God has given us the Spirit of self-discipline (2 Timothy 1:7). Think of things that honor God. God has prosperous plans for you, plans to give you hope and a future (Jeremiah 29:11). When circumstances get bad, remind yourself of God's goodness and His promises. The Bible says in Philippians 4:8,

"Whatever is true, whatever is noble, whatever is right, whatever is pure, whatever is lovely, whatever is admirable—if anything is excellent or praiseworthy—think about such things." We are called to think of pure, noble, and right things. It is possible to align our thinking with the word of God, dear friend. The Holy Spirit is your guide and helper. Jesus is your High Priest. God, our Father, is always for you.

Your Shepherd:

One of the names of God is Jehovah Rohi, which means 'the Lord is my Shepherd' (Psalm 23). As we all know, a shepherd is someone who takes care of his sheep. He leads them to green, abundant pastures and water. He protects his sheep from wild animals (1 Samuel 17:34-35). He knows every one of his sheep because they are precious to him. He guards them at all times. When you think of the Lord as your Shepherd, I want you to know He is a very personal God. Now, don't think of Him as the Shepherd of all Christians. At this moment, I want you to think of Him as exclusively *'your Shepherd.'* We often fail to see Him as our Shepherd, especially in our thought life. Your Shepherd is for you and not against you (1 Peter 5:6-7).

Another translation of *Rohi* is 'companion' or 'friend.' He is a very intimate God. Your Shepherd wants to commune with you. He already knows your thoughts and struggles. He wants you to release your thinking to Him, so He may walk with you in all your battles. We are described as joint-heirs with Christ (Romans 8:7). He's the same God who called Abraham His *friend* and David a *man after His (God's) own heart*. Surrender your thoughts to your Shepherd. He will see you through life's days and stick to you closer than a brother (Proverbs 18:24).

The Prophet Elijah is one of the mightiest prophets of all time. Ahab became King during the days of Elijah and married an evil woman, Jezebel. Jezebel wasted no time turning Ahab and the people of Israel to Baal worship. The Lord spoke to King Ahab through Elijah, saying that there will be neither dew nor rain for the next few years because of his idol worship (1 Kings 17:1). After delivering the Lord's word, Elijah ran away.

We see that God directed him to a place called Kerith Ravine, where He fed Elijah bread and meat twice daily, in the morning and the evening, through ravens. After a while, the brook dried up, and God asked Elijah to move to another region. The Lord led Elijah to a widow's house in Zarephath (1 Kings 17:7). As he arrived in the town, he saw the widow gathering sticks and asking her for food and water. The widow says, "I don't have any bread—only a handful of flour in a jar and a little olive oil in a jug. I am gathering a few sticks to take home and make a meal for myself and my son, that we may eat it—and die (1 Kings 17:12)." The widow was at the end of her rope.

I want you to notice how hopeless her situation was. She was at the end of her rope because her circumstances were excruciating. Her thinking transcended from negativity to absolute hopelessness; she saw no point in life anymore. So many of us are trapped in situations where everything seems hopeless, but let me tell you that God's got you. The Lord says in Isaiah 41:10, "So do not fear, for I am with you; do not be dismayed, for I am your God. I will strengthen you and help you; I will uphold you with my righteous right hand." He is always with you.

Elijah then told the widow, "The jar of flour will not be used up, and the jug of oil will not run dry until the day the Lord sends rain on the land." Thus, the widow was able to bake bread for Elijah, herself, and also her sons. The jar of flour was never used up, and the jug of oil never ran out as Elijah prophesized (1 Kings 17:16).

Three years after this incident, God spoke to Elijah, saying, "Go and present yourself to Ahab, and I will send rain on the land." So Elijah went to Ahab and told him to gather all the prophets of Baal on Mount Carmel. They were to build an altar and call out to their Gods (Baal) to send fire to burn up the offerings. The prophets were then gathered and were given a bullock. They put it on the altar and called on the name of Baal from morning till noon. After that, they danced around the altar and slashed themselves with swords and spears, yet there was no response.

It was evening time, and Elijah called all the people and started preparing the altar of the Lord. He laid 12 stones for the 12 tribes of Israel, arranged the wood around the altar, and spread the meat on the wood. He then poured four large jars of water on the altar three times, filling the trench around the altar. He then cried out to the Lord, and fire fell from heaven. The fire consumed the trench's wood, stones, soil, and water. The people were astonished and came back to the Lord. Elijah then told the Israelites to kill all the prophets of Baal. After this, there was rain for several years.

One person who was unhappy with this was Jezebel. She vowed to avenge the death of the prophets of Baal by killing Elijah. Elijah was afraid and fled to the wilderness in Beersheba, where he cried out to the Lord, saying, "I have had enough, Lord, take my life; I am no better than my ancestors." Elijah was beyond just negative thinking; he was utterly depressed. He intimately knew the Lord all the days of his life yet could not have faith in the Lord. He chose to trust his circumstances rather than the Lord.

But Jehovah Rohi never leaves his children alone. He knows that our minds are frail. We see that the Lord put Elijah to sleep and then sent an angel to give him food and water. Jehovah Rohi, the intimate one, never left Elijah. Despite his negative thoughts and circumstances, God was his Shepherd. Elijah traveled for forty days and reached Horeb.

At Horeb, God appeared to Elijah. At first, there was a mighty wind that tore the mountains apart. After that, there was an earthquake followed by a fire, and the Lord was in neither of them. Then there was a gentle whisper, and the Lord spoke to Elijah. I want you to notice that God's word came to Elijah as a gentle whisper. God's word is a weapon against the lies of the enemy. Even if your situation worsens by the day and your mind seems to whisper the most negative of things, remember that the Word of God (the word of truth) is always with you. Jehovah Rohi, the intimate one, never left Elijah. He showed up the most glorious way when Elijah needed Him the most. Your Shepherd will never leave you alone. He is waiting in the gentleness of every day; He stays in the silent place. Seek Him now.

Renew your mind:

Before you think about this step, let me tell you that it is possible. The Bible says in Romans 12:2, "Do not conform to the pattern of this world but be transformed by the renewing of your mind. Then you can test and approve what God's will is—his good, pleasing and perfect will." Let me start by explaining why doing the will of God is literally life-giving. It isn't easy; it is definitely out of our 'comfort zones,' but perfect and right for us. Jesus said in Matthew 7:21, "Not everyone who says to me, 'Lord, Lord,' will enter the kingdom of heaven, but only the one who does the will of my Father who is in heaven." Only those who do the will of God will go to heaven and be with the Lord forever. This is why praying for God's will and living in His will is of utmost importance to believers.

The second thing we notice here is that we are not to

conform to the patterns of this world. Self-will is deceptive and creeps into the smallest of things. The world calls us to live our way and do our own things. The world wants us to conform to their methods and philosophies. The devil will draw you to the carnal desires of the mind or flesh (Ephesians 2:3). Satan usually uses our personality defects or emotional turmoil to blur us from seeing the will of God. The devil often uses unresolved conflict or childhood trauma to lure us into its traps. It is usually easy to confuse ourselves over God's desires for our lives and fleshly desires. Falling prey to our fleshly desires is a battle we must fight every day. The patterns of this world are enticing and attractive, but we are to reject them.

The third point is, *'be transformed by the renewing of your mind.'* To kick off this step, I want you to consider your answers to the retrospective questions in Chapter 3. Now on a scale of 1 to 10, one being extremely bad and ten being excellent, what is your mind spiritually? Be honest with yourself while scoring your mind because I know for a fact that as human beings, we all need to be transformed by the renewing of our minds because of our carnal minds. If you've scored pretty high, kudos to you on having a healthy mind, but if you've scored low or you're skeptical about your mind, there is freedom for you. Here are a few practical ways by which you can renew your mind according to the word of God:

1. **Forget the past, focus on God's victories:** The past has a way of coming back to us repeatedly. But the Bible says in Philippians 3:13-14, "Forgetting what is behind and straining toward what is ahead, I press on toward the goal to win the prize for which God has called me heavenward in Christ Jesus." Let me tell you that your failures do not

define you; Jesus Christ does. Before God called him, the apostle Paul hunted and murdered Christians. He had an appalling record and could let this define him, but he chose to trust God instead. He left his past in God's hands and decided to press on for God's glory. As a result, God forgave Paul completely and renewed his mind. This victory is yours too, dear friend. God is able! He is always victorious and can save us when calling Him out. So when your circumstances get hard and your thinking seems to take off, dwell on God's victories in your life.

2. **The weapon of prayer:** Prayer is one of the most potent weapons given to us by God. The Bible says in Philippians 4:6-7, "Do not be anxious about anything, but in every situation, by prayer and petition, with thanksgiving, present your requests to God. And the peace of God, which transcends all understanding, will guard your hearts and your minds in Christ Jesus." Paul asks all believers to pray at all times; pray through every situation. When you approach the throne of God in prayer, give thanks to Him before you bring up your petition. When Jesus prayed, He started by acknowledging God's greatness and holiness (Matthew 6:9). Then, approach your Father's throne and tell Him your problem. Finally, pray that the Lord gives you, in increasing measures, the Spirit of truth to combat negative thinking.

3. **Meditate on God's word: God:** The word of God is a double-edged sword that cuts the spirit of man (Hebrews 4:12). The Psalmist says in Psalms 119:11, "I have stored up your word in my heart, that I might not sin against you." The word of God

is the sword of the Spirit (Ephesians 6:170, which is a part of the armor that God has given His children. This sword is a weapon of offense; it is used to attack the enemy. Our minds must be brought under Christ to align with God's will. By meditating on God's word day and night (Joshua 1:8), we are filling our minds with the sanctifying truth. The truth is now a weapon of war that can be used to attack the enemy. The word of God is more precious than the air we breathe or the food we eat; it is rightfully called the bread of life (Matthew 4:4). Therefore, a believer needs to learn to utilize the weapons of warfare that God has given them because spiritual warfare is real.

4. **Set your mind on the truth:** The Bible says in Colossians 3:2-4, "Set your minds on things above, not on earthly things. For you died, and your life is now hidden with Christ in God. When Christ, who is your life, appears, then you also will appear with him in glory." As believers, we are dead to the world. I know this seems a bit too much, but Paul asks us to put to death any impure and evil thoughts. As children of God, our home is heaven; this world is just a temporary residency. You and I live in the resurrection of Christ. We have no business with the darkness; as such, we must daily forsake unrighteous and unhealthy thoughts because we are dead to this world. So how do we set our minds on the truth? This is done through the Holy Spirit. Only God can change our minds and draw us to Himself. We can do our part by meditating on His word as often as possible and praying at all times.

5. **Selective thinking:** We are called to think of things that are true, noble, honorable, just, lovely, and pure (Philippians 4:6). We studied this verse in the previous section to change our focus. True thoughts stem from the word of God and His promises. Satan is the father of lies and deception, and we demolish demonic strongholds using the word of truth. Nobel thoughts are rooted in God's promises. You need to exercise your faith to think these thoughts. The Bible says in 2 Corinthians 4:28, "While we look not at the things which are seen, but at the things which are not seen; for the things which are seen are temporal, but the things which are not seen are eternal." Therefore, our thoughts must be fixed on the hope of eternal salvation. Righteousness produces righteousness, and just thoughts are often rooted in God's character that has been placed on us. Paul warns believers in Romans 12:21, "Do not be overcome by evil, but overcome evil with good." As children of the living God, we must do what is right; we are smeared with His goodness.
6. **Role models:** Paul says in 1 Corinthians 11:1, "Follow my example, as I follow the example of Christ." Role models are positive motivators and have already walked the path ahead of us. The book of Hebrews talks about a cloud of witnesses (Hebrews 12:1) that have gone ahead of us in whose footsteps we can walk (Hebrews 11). Children look up to their parents, who are their primary role models. Their lives are shaped by the actions and choices of their parents because they choose to imitate them. In the same way, human beings were made to follow and mimic others. Let

me tell you that Christ is and will always be our absolute and primary role model. Our selection of role models will influence our values and the way we live. Before you pick a role model, you must measure the person against God's standards which we've already seen in Philippians 4:8. These standards call for a person who is *true*, which means they must be free of falsehood, malice, and deceit. The person must be *just*, which means the person must be obedient to God's word and have good moral conduct. The person must be *noble* by nature and a seeker of God's righteousness. Her motives must be *pure* and blameless. She must be *virtuous*, *lovely*, and *praiseworthy*. Above all, the person must honor God in everything they do. Such a noteworthy person who can be followed as a role model.

7. **Positive affirmations rooted in the word of God:** Our thoughts define our life, so what we think is who we will become. Positive affirmations used by believers must be rooted in the word of God. To use them, we must exercise our faith in God. Regular positive affirmations are rooted in one's faith in herself, but Biblical affirmations are based on complete faith and dependence on God. Jesus said in Matthew 17:20, "Because you have so little faith. Truly I tell you, if you have faith as small as a mustard seed, you can say to this mountain, 'Move from here to there,' and it will move. Nothing will be impossible for you." Feed your mind faith. Feed it the word of God because this is where faith comes from (2 Corinthians 5:17). Eliminate unbelief by asking the Holy Spirit to strengthen you in your weaknesses. It is important to

remember that prayer and positive affirmations go hand in hand. God wants us to pray to Him through every situation. Pray to Him for greater faith because He will give it to you in increasing measures. When going through a trial, speak the word of God out loud. Speak out affirmations that are based on God's word. Resist the devil in this way, and he will flee. A few Biblical affirmations are given below:

- I am the daughter of a King (1 Peter 2:9)
- I am more than a conqueror in Christ (Romans 8:31)
- I am strong and courageous (Deuteronomy 31:6)
- I am completely forgiven and new (2 Corinthians 5:17)
- God covers me with His feathers; no harm will befall me (Psalm 91:4)
- My future is filled with hope (Jeremiah 29:11)
- God is fighting my battles (Deuteronomy 20:4)
- Fear does not own me; I am filled with love and the power of God (2 Timothy 1:7)
- I live in His peace (Philippians 4:6-8)
- I have God's armor (Ephesians 6)
- I am an overcomer (I Corinthians 15:57)
- Nothing can ever separate me from Christ (Romans 8:28)

Scriptures to conquer negative thoughts:
Here are a few scriptures that you can write down, memorize, print out as a reminder, or journal:

1. Philippians 4:7: And the peace of God, which transcends all understanding, will guard your hearts and your minds in Christ Jesus.
2. Matthew 10:30-31: And even the very hairs of your head are all numbered. So don't be afraid; you are worth more than many sparrows.
3. Psalm 94:19: When anxiety was great within me, your consolation brought me joy.
4. 1 Thessalonians 5:16-18: Rejoice always, pray continually, give thanks in all circumstances; for this is God's will for you in Christ Jesus.
5. Philippians 4:8: Whatever is true, whatever is noble, whatever is right, whatever is pure, whatever is lovely, whatever is admirable—if anything is excellent or praiseworthy—think about such things.
6. Hebrews 4:12: For the word of God is living and active and sharper than any two-edged sword, and piercing as far as the division of soul and spirit, of both joints and marrow, and able to judge the thoughts and intentions of the heart.

5

TRANSFORM WHAT YOU SAY GOD'S WAY

"Watch over your heart with all diligence, for from it flow the springs of life."

— PROVERBS 4:23

*L*ife is war. John Piper once said, "Until you know that life is war, you cannot know what life is for." Did you know that Christian life is war? What is the purpose of life? Have you ever asked yourself this question? Are you living in God's will? Have you been honoring Him in all things? Before we jump into the chapter, I want to talk about one of the many names of our God, *Jehovah Nissi*, which means 'the Lord my banner of victory.' Do you believe that the Lord is victorious in your life? Do you believe that He fights your battles? More importantly, is your faith pure and strong? Take a moment to dwell on these questions.

One day, Jesus decided to send His disciples ahead of Him

because He wanted to get alone and spend time in prayer. Late in the night, the disciples were on the boat and far away from the shore, but Jesus decided to walk toward them. He started walking on water, and suddenly, Peter wanted to walk toward Him. Jesus asked him to come. Then we see what happened in Matthew 14:29, "Then Peter got down out of the boat, walked on the water and came toward Jesus. But when he saw the wind, he was afraid and, beginning to sink, cried out, "Lord, save me!" Peter could not walk on water until he fixed his eyes on Christ. Once he looked at his circumstances and turned his eyes to the wind, his faith started to wear out. He started to sink. As long as he fixated his eyes on Jehovah Nissi, he was on the winning side and was able to walk on water. As the story continues, we see that Jesus caught him and said, "You of little faith, why did you doubt?" How is your story, friend? We're halfway through the book now. Have you made any substantial changes? Have you been exercising your faith and shunning negative thoughts?

The practice of Christian mindfulness:

Sin is everywhere. Unless the light of God's salvation comes to us, we are covered in the darkness (Isaiah 60:1). Elisabeth Elliot once said, "We want to avoid suffering, death, sin, ashes. But we live in a world crushed and broken and torn, a world God Himself visited to redeem. We receive his poured-out life, and being allowed the high privilege of suffering with Him, may then pour ourselves out for others." We live in a broken and crushed world where suffering is inevitable. But the question here is, why is it unavoidable? Because we live in sin, sin is in our very DNA.

This sin breaks our minds. The prophet Jeremiah summed this up pretty well when he says in Jeremiah 17:9, "The heart is deceitful above all things and beyond cure. Who can understand it?" Our minds lie to us quite often. We sometimes convince ourselves of things that aren't even happening, and other times, we tend to ignore our circumstances and hide from them. We lie to ourselves. This is why we need to question every thought that comes to mind. Not even half of our thoughts are usually healthy.

Satan is (obviously) the father of lies (John 8:44). He is the king of deception. Not a word from his mouth is true. We've seen how demons attack our minds and spew their lies and hatred all over us in previous chapters. If he can get you to fall into one of his small 'thought traps,' he can get you to sin against God. When God says something, the devil counters it with thoughts of 'what if?' or 'are you sure?' His strategy is one of planting small seeds of doubt. A little bit of doubt is enough to take over our fragile broken minds.

How do we combat these lies with a broken mind? We can do so by practicing Christian mindfulness. Before we get into the meaning of 'Christian mindfulness,' I'm sure we all know what mindfulness is. Jon Kabat-Zinn, a professor in medicine, says that mindfulness is "the awareness that emerges through paying attention on purpose, in the present moment, and nonjudgmentally to the unfolding of experience moment by moment." There are two components in this definition: paying careful attention or consciously scrutinizing one's thoughts. The second component to notice here is 'being non-judgmental.' One has to pay careful attention to their thoughts by being compassionate and empathetic to oneself. It is also important to note that overindulging in mindfulness promotes a high degree of self-focus, which is unhealthy. Your focus must be on Christ. There is a fine line between healthy mindfulness and obsession with oneself.

The Bible says in 2 Corinthians 10:3-4, "For though we live in the world, we do not wage war as the world does. The weapons we fight with are not the weapons of the world. On the contrary, they have divine power to demolish strongholds." This verse states that we do not fight against other human beings, money, or animals, but we fight against powers and principalities in the spiritual realm. We can destroy these demonic strongholds in the name of Jesus Christ. Demons flee in Christ's name; they cannot stand in His presence.

Mental attacks from the devil can be in several forms. The most common type of mental attack is the mental attack of fear (2 Timothy 1:7). The second type of mental attack is the attack of the lust for the flesh (1 John 2:16). The third type of attack is the mental attack of sudden anger (Matthew 5:22). The fourth type of attack is the attack of mental oppression (Acts 10:38). The fifth type of mental attack is the attack of condemnation from sin (1 John 3:20-22). Negative thinking can be camouflaged in any of these forms. Are you falling prey to these attacks, dear friend?

Developing self-compassion:

I want you to ponder on something for a minute. I want you to think about the last two weeks. How were they? Did you have good days? Or were they bad days? Were you kind to yourself? How was your self-talk?

As we saw above, cultivating Christian mindfulness can be very helpful in making our thoughts obedient to Christ. The Bible speaks about how Jesus always had compassion for the crowds while preaching in many instances (Matthew 15:32, Luke 7:13, Matthew 9:36, Matthew 14:14, Matthew 20:34). The heart of God is full of compassion (Psalm 116:5). The Bible says in Lamentations 3:22-23, "Because of the Lord's great love we are not consumed, for his compassions never fail. They are new every morning; great is your faithfulness." His compassions are eternal and immeasurable. The

Bible tells us numerous stories of God's unending compassion. He looks at you and me with infinite love.

One of my favorite Biblical examples of Jesus' compassion is the death of Lazarus. Lazarus was the brother of Mary and Martha. When Jesus arrived at Bethany, Lazarus was dead for almost four days and was buried in the tomb. Mary and Martha were utterly broken and in great pain. The Bible says in John 11:33-35, "When Jesus saw her weeping, and the Jews who had come along with her also weeping, he was deeply moved in spirit and troubled. "Where have you laid him?" he asked, "Come and see, Lord," they replied. Jesus wept." Jesus was moved by their pain and had a great deal of compassion for them. He cried. God cried, dear friends. Can you believe this? The great God who knit time and space into being and formed all of the oceans, trees, and animals cried at the death of his friend. This gives us a little glimpse into the heart of God. He is filled with love and compassion for His children.

The greatest act of compassion was when Jesus went to the cross for you and me. He gave up everything for us. His sacrifice is the most remarkable example of compassion. His grace is being poured out on us in increasing measures (Ephesians 2:7). If God's grace is being poured out in such amounts with immense compassion, this raises the question of being compassionate to ourselves. Are we practicing self-compassion? Many of us are moved with compassion when we see others in pain or suffering, but are we compassionate to ourselves when we need it?

I've been hugely guilty of constantly condemning myself in my mind. There were days when I was very hard on myself. Even when the Lord forgave me, I lived in the light of my forgiven sins. I wasn't able to forgive myself. It is one of my most significant weaknesses, to be honest. This is the tragedy of the human mind. We choose to believe that everyone needs grace, but when it comes to ourselves, we miserably fail at being compassionate or forgiving. When God has let it go, you must too. The Bible says in Psalms 103:12, "As far as the east is from the west, so far has he removed our transgressions from us." This is how compassionate and forgiving God is towards His children.

I agree that we are held to very high standards as redeemed saints of the Most High God, but does this mean we beat ourselves up for everything? By no means! To be compassionate to oneself is to accept and receive God's love. Self-compassion is rooted in God's compassion for us. The heavy burden of shame and self-condemnation will wear you out. Ask God for forgiveness and bring it under His control when your thoughts seem to haunt you. Surrender them to Him because when we are weak, we can live in God's strength (2 Corinthians 12:9-11). When God forgives you, learn to forgive yourself too. It is not healthy to keep count of all your wrongdoings when Christ forgave you. Learn to dwell in His forgiveness and peace.

Let us consider a woman struggling with lustful or impure thoughts from time to time. She finds it difficult to control her eyes, and her brain automatically signals her to look at a certain attractive person. She then falls into an unending spiral of negative thoughts and keeps condemning herself. What does the Bible have to say about this? Jesus said that if we look at someone lustfully, we are committing adultery. There is nothing wrong with just looking at a person (Matthew 5:28). There is a distinct difference between admiring a pretty person (pure thoughts) and lusting after them. If you're struggling with impure or lustful thoughts, I urge you to bring them under Christ's dominion. Fast and pray about it because God will change and renew your mind.

A lot of times, our scrutiny and self-condemnation result in self-hatred. I urge you to dwell on the kindness and compassion of God our Father. The Bible says in 1 John 1:3, "See what great love the Father has lavished on us, that we should be called children of God! And that is what we are!" His love and compassion are on you, dear friend. Live under the shadow of the character of God.

Start by acknowledging the fact that you are human and flawed. Sin is a part of our very nature (Psalm 51:5). You need to understand that God made you, and He thoroughly knows you. There is nothing you've done that is hidden from Him (Hebrews 4:13). Other people don't define you; God does. Take responsibility for your flaws and go to the throne of God, who is rich in compassion. God is your comforter; rely on His comfort and know that you are seen.

How to transform your words and win the battle:

To transform your words and your thoughts, start by surrendering to God. I have repeated this quite a bit, but this sheds some light on how important it is to offer everything to God. Only God can create lasting and concrete changes. Relying on the Holy Spirit in all you think is key to breaking ground. Here is a step-by-step guide to winning this battle:

1. Do not believe everything you say to yourself: I'm usually haunted by thoughts that attack my self-esteem like 'You're not good enough,' 'You've sinned, God doesn't love you anymore,' or 'You will never go to heaven.' Or 'There is no hope for you.' I know these are lies, yet I sometimes succumb to them. It is normal and quite natural to think they must be valid when thoughts like this attack. You and I are human. But if these thoughts attack you regularly, take them captive. Combat them with the truth of the Word and condemn such thoughts. The devil is a defeated foe, and we must show him his place. Choose to put your trust in the Word of God rather than what your mind tells you. Actively practice fighting these thoughts with the sword of the Spirit (Ephesians 6:17).

2. Guard your mind against garbage: Let me start by asking you this question, what are you feeding your mind? Are you feeding it the Word of God, or are you feeding it the words of the world? I cannot stress how important it is to store God's Word in your heart (Psalm 119:11). As human beings, we are weak and susceptible to all kinds of mental attacks. A wise man once said, "Be careful the friends you choose, for you will become like them." I couldn't agree more! If you surround yourself with the world, its voice will get louder than God's. If you surround yourself with the children of God, you will be enlightened.

After a few years of marriage, I couldn't believe how much of my thinking had changed. I started talking and joking like my partner. I started doing a lot of life just like he did. You become a lot like the people around you. The Bible says in Proverbs 13:20, "Walk with the wise and become wise, for a companion of fools suffers harm." The people you spend time with will influence you in the most remarkable ways. Choose wisely. It is essential to guard our minds against the garbage of the world.

It is imperative to put on the complete *Armor of God* (Ephesians 6). Paul says in Ephesians 6:17, "Take the helmet of salvation and the sword of the Spirit, which is the word of God." Let me begin with the helmet of salvation. In ancient times, Roman soldiers used to wear helmets made out of copper and iron. War is brutal, and these helmets protect the head from serious injury. The top part of the helmet was round and bowl-like, with a brow guard that projected out of the top. They protected the top of the head and also the forehead. The helmet's left and right sides had movable flaps that protected the cheeks and the sides of the face from injury. This helmet protected the mind on the front, side, and back. Every Christian must put on their helmet of salvation. When you receive salvation and have an assurance of it, don't let the fiery darts (lies) of the enemy get into your head. Use your helmet (your evidence of salvation) to rebuke the devil and his attacks against your mind.

In the same way, the sword of the Spirit is a weapon of offense. The Word of God is defined as a sword in Hebrews 4:12, "For the word of God is alive and active. Sharper than any double-edged sword, it penetrates even to dividing soul and spirit, joints and marrow; it judges the thoughts and attitudes of the heart." It is important to note that it is a *double-edged sword* with two edges. God speaks the first edge (His Word), and the second is the word of our testimony (Revelations 12:11). We must exercise the authority of the Word of God. Claim it and speak it out loud; this is how we defeat the devil. The Holy Spirit will fight for you by bringing up God's Word in your time of need. He will remind you of it. This is where faith comes to play. Faith comes by hearing God's Word; unless you have faith in Him, you cannot exercise His authority over the enemy's attacks. You are simply not strong enough.

The other vital weapons of warfare are given in Ephesians 6:14-16, "Stand firm then, with the belt of truth buckled around your waist, with the breastplate of righteousness in place, and with your feet fitted with the readiness that comes from the gospel of peace. In addition to all this, take up the shield of faith, with which you can extinguish all the flaming arrows of the evil one." I urge you to put on the complete armor of God, dear friend. Like I said before, the Christian life is war, and you won't win the battle in your strength. God has already provided us with His weapons; you need to put them on and fight the war.

The Bible says in proverbs 15:14, "A wise person is hungry for knowledge, while the fool feeds on trash." Don't be a people pleaser and listen to all the trash around you. What you feed your brain is what it will grow on. Feed it love, hope, and faith. Don't feed it junk or toxic thoughts. Feed your mind God's Word at all times. Psalms 101:3 says, "I will not set before my eyes anything that is worthless." Anything that doesn't glorify God is worthless. Anything that causes you to sin is useless. Be careful of what you let into your life because it will define your thought life.

3. **Keep learning:** According to Rick Warren, there are five levels of learning. Based on James 1:22-25, which says, "Do not merely listen to the word, and so deceive yourselves. Do what it says. Anyone who listens to the word but does not do what it says is like someone who looks at his face in a mirror and, after looking at himself, goes away and immediately forgets what he looks like. But whoever looks intently into the perfect law that gives freedom and continues in it not forgetting what they have heard, but doing it—they will be blessed in what they do." All these steps are based on 'knowing,' 'being,' and 'doing' the Word of God according to him. Let us look at these steps individually:

- **Knowledge:** The Word of God is our daily bread, and Jesus asks us to pray that we are given our daily bread in 'The Lord's Prayer.' Knowing the Word of God is crucial. Jesus said in Matthew 22:19, "You are in error because you do not know the Scriptures or the power of God." Faith is built when we read the Word of God. Without His Word, we can't grow in faith. Without faith, we cannot please God.
- **Perspective:** In times of crisis, our perspective is essential. The Israelites developed an attitude of grumbling and not trusting God even when they saw Him constantly work wonders (Exodus 16). When your thoughts start to get negative, eat the Word of God and adopt the proper perspective.

God is working for you, and you must receive His revelations through the Word. When Jesus was on earth, the Bible says that He kept growing in wisdom and stature (Luke 2:52). In the same way, as children of God, we are to pray for and grow in wisdom.

- **Conviction:** The definition of conviction is firmly held or believed in. It is the practice of holding onto something no matter what. Even if your circumstance and everything around you scream the opposite, you still believe and hold onto your conviction. Job was a fantastic example of someone who held onto his conviction. Even after all that he went through, he says, "Though he slay me, yet will I trust in him." This is the faith and conviction we need. When a negative thought attacks you, the conviction of the Word of God must be stronger than the thought itself; then, you will be able to overcome it.

- **Character:** Character is built on the back of habits. This is why developing Godly habits is of utmost importance. The Bible says in Galatians 5:22-23, "But the fruit of the Spirit is love, joy, peace, forbearance, kindness, goodness, faithfulness, gentleness, and self-control. Against such things, there is no law." The fruits of the Spirit need to become a part of our character. Unless and until we practice these regularly, we cannot make a habit out of them. As we go ahead in life, we need to become more like Christ. These fruits reflect Christ in us, and we must gain them in increasing measures. Our helper, the Holy Spirit, will guide us into this knowledge. Character is who we are, and we get better at

fighting our battles when we become more like Christ.
- **Skill:** Anything that is perfected becomes a skill. It becomes a way of life. In the same way, the Word of God needs to become our way of life. We need to embody it. How is this done? By habitually reading the Word of God, praying, fasting, and seeking God in everything. The Bible says in Ecclesiastes 10:10, "If the ax is dull and its edge unsharpened, more strength is needed, but skill will bring success." Our words must turn into actions. Without actions, the words are just empty words that have no power—developing skills in living the Word of God helps us fight our battles effectively. When we master the fight, we can also uphold those around us and stand in the gap.

4. Allow God to work His power on your imagination: God stretches our imagination. How does He do this? By testing us. As a result of the trials we go through, our faith in Him will increase, and this is how He pushes our imagination. Let me talk to you about the story of Abraham. When God called Abram, He didn't give him a destination (Genesis 12:1). He just gave Him a promise or a revelation. Abram had to look at God's revelation, imagine it, and keep his eyes on the Lord. God stretched Abram's imagination throughout the journey. God is glorified through our faith, which is how we fight our battles. We also know that it is impossible to please God without faith (Hebrews 11:6). God pulls us through our trials, and when our faith is stretched, we trust in His Word more and more. We begin to understand and exercise the power of His Word.

5. Speak God's Word: Finally, Speak out His Word. We've seen that we can overcome the devil's lies by the blood of the

Lamb and the word of our testimony (Revelation 12:11). So for every negative thought that comes to mind, fight it with the Word of God. Fight it with His revelations. The weapons have already been given to you. It is time you put on the armor of God and battle the enemy, dear friend.

6

THE EMOTIONAL BEING IN YOU

"A joyful heart is good medicine, but a crushed spirit dries up the bones."

— PROVERBS 17:22

A few years ago, I came home after a long and tiring workday. I was utterly exhausted and just wanted to crash. My rabbit Max went on a wild goose chase and broke many delicate things in the house. As I entered the house, I was shocked. My sense of shock then turned to anger as I saw all was destroyed. My thoughts took off, and in that moment of rage, I really couldn't control them. I could feel the anger burning through my skin. We all have days where situations really get to us. It is normal to have such days. I know how it feels to have no control of your emotions at times. In such situations, you need to let yourself run with your feelings. It is okay to have such moments; you're only human.

What are emotions?

Let me start by saying that we are all emotional beings. As we have been created in the image of God, we have emotions just like Him. The difference between God and us is that He is absolutely perfect (Psalms 18:30), whereas we are fallen beings. The Merriam-Webster dictionary defines emotions as "a conscious mental reaction (such as anger or fear) subjectively experienced as a strong feeling usually directed toward a specific object and typically accompanied by physiological and behavioral changes in the body." Emotions are usually reactions to the situations around us. They are formed in our minds and expressed through our actions. When we feel emotions, we judge the events around us and react to them.

Sometimes, we don't realize that we've judged something and emotionally respond to it because it happens swiftly. But most of the time, we process the situation around us before reacting to it. We examine everything and weigh it against our logic before responding to it in the form of action. As we know, emotions are generally of two types: positive and negative. Positive emotions include happiness, joy, excitement, and hope, whereas negative emotions involve feeling sadness, anxiety, fear, worry, and guilt. We judge circumstances or situations based on our past experiences. Feelings of hope, joy, and happiness are in anticipation of something good. But feelings of guilt or sorrow are consequences of either wrongdoing or something bad in some cases.

As such, emotions are simply just not feeling. They don't always spring out of our minds. Instead, they start from an intersection between the body and mind. Sometimes we react to what happens around us. For example, the death of a loved one brings out emotions of sorrow and heartache. It has nothing to do with something we did or thought; instead, the circumstance defined the emotion of the hour. Other times, the events around us are consequences of our feelings.

For example, you've been stressed out at work and subconsciously take it out on your partner. This can and will strain your relationship with him; in this case, the circumstance was a consequence of an emotion you were feeling.

How are emotions related to our faith? How are emotions that Christians feel different from those felt by the world? The Bible is filled with emotion, from the Old to the New Testament. For example, the fear of the Lord is a good emotion and an essential requirement for all believers (Deuteronomy 6:13). In stark contrast, God asks His children not to fear in times of trouble (Isaiah 41:10). Likewise, anger is a sin (Ephesians 4:31), yet God has righteous anger (Romans 1:18).

David went through depression (Psalm 42). His life was full of pain, and he always sang songs of lament. His emotions were directly related to his faith in God. Even through challenging circumstances and depression, he chose to put his complete trust in the Lord. All of his psalms talk about the reality of life and end in a declaration of faith. Elijah begged the Lord to take his life when things got complicated (1 Kings 19). Job cursed the day he was born because he was weighed down by his circumstances (Job 3), yet he completely trusted God. The teacher of Ecclesiastes was a man of great wisdom, riches, and honor, yet his words spoke of the harsh reality of life, and he called everything meaningless (Ecclesiastes 2).

David's circumstances were a million times worse than that of Solomon. Yet, we see that David still praised God through them and gave Him all the glory. On the other hand, Solomon had a very wise mind and felt things on a deeper level. Even though his circumstances were not dire, he called life 'meaningless.' Elijah had just won a victory when he cried out to God to take his life. He defeated the prophets of Baal and had them slain (1 Kings 18,19). On the other hand, Job lost everything. He lost his wife, children, wealth, and all he had (Job 1). He cursed the day of his birth yet did not utter a word against God.

Life is hard. Often, our circumstances weigh us down, and everything gets heavy. People's experience is quite diverse, and we all react to situations differently. Some of us go through an immense amount of pain in our life, whereas some of us aren't crushed to such a degree. Different people react in different ways to such events. Some people take it to heart and get deeply hurt, whereas others move on easily. There is a vast diversity in emotions among human beings.

The level of emotions felt by each person is quite contrasting to that felt by another. What does the Bible have to say about such a broad spectrum of emotions? How should we deal with different emotions? The Bible says in Proverbs 26:4-5, "Do not answer a fool according to his folly, or you yourself will be just like him. Answer a fool according to his folly, or he will be wise in his own eyes." Words that fit perfectly into some situations don't usually work in others. In the same way, there are no specific commandments given in the Bible regarding human emotions. God understands what all of us feel, and He sees our pain.

Certain circumstances call for rejoicing, whereas others call for weeping (Romans 12:15). As seen above, our minds are broken because we live in a fallen world. There are times when we cannot control our emotions or days when we don't know how to react to the situation. One such incident can be seen during the time of Joseph. He was sold into slavery by his brothers and purchased by Potiphar, the captain of Pharoah's guard (Genesis 39). Potiphar's wife wrongly accused Joseph of harassing her; we all know this was a lie. But Potiphar was enraged and threw Joseph into prison. From Potiphar's perspective, his emotional response was correct and justified. But, when you see the entire story, we know his reaction was negative. So, my point is that there will be times when we think we are right and justified in responding to circumstances, but God only knows the ultimate reality.

A lot of us believe in perfection. When we apply this trait of perfection emotionally, it can lead to disastrous results. When we try and try in our strength to perfect our emotions, we fight a losing battle. This is why we need the grace of God every single day. The prophet Jeremiah sings about God's mercy in Lamentations 3:22-23, saying, "The steadfast love of the Lord never ceases; his mercies never come to an end; they are new every morning; great is your faithfulness." He gives us fresh mercy every day, which is why we need the Gospel daily. Always remember that in our moment of weakness, God is strong. You can call out to Him for help in the day of trouble (Joel 2:12).

Our faith keeps increasing as we get deeper in our relationship with Christ. The root of our emotion lies in our evaluations of the past, present, and future. The way we view the world is how we perceive it to be. We react to events in life according to these preconceived notions. Our faith is directly related to the emotions we feel because these emotions drive our bodily actions. The actions we take will define our tomorrow. Hence, our faith is a product of our feelings. But we also need to consider the move of the Holy Spirit in our lives, which is supernatural. There will be times when God moves our emotions, and we respond to circumstances around us in the shadow of His grace and mercy. This is why we need to pray that He gives us His mercy in our weak moments.

Paul talks about his weakness in the book of Corinthians and says that he asked God to remove this particular weakness as it haunts him. But we see God's response in 2 Corinthians 12:9, "But he said to me, "My grace is sufficient for you, for my power is made perfect in weakness." Therefore I will boast all the more gladly about my weaknesses so that Christ's power may rest on me." This is the grace that has been given to us. Even in our weakness, God is in control. God's got you! He has you covered under the shadow of His wings (Psalm 91:4). He has paved the way, and you can find peace from your worries, anxieties, fears. Rest in Him.

Feel the emotion, do not be ruled by it:

One pleasant August day, I was sitting by the window and looking at the rain. It was past lunchtime, and my partner ran out to grab some ingredients to cook dinner. You see, it was date night, and He was supposed to pamper me. So I just sat down and decided to absorb the beauty of the thundering rain. I was deep in thought when suddenly I felt this darkness descend onto me. My heart started beating out of control; I almost thought it would fall out of my chest. I was scared to death, and I couldn't stop shaking. To top it all off, I was alone.

Immediately, out of nowhere, I felt this urge to use the Word of God as a weapon against this darkness. So I spoke the Word of God out loud and the darkness slowly lifted. If you've been struggling with overwhelming emotions, there is hope for you. The following technique can be used to bring it under control:

1. **Accept your emotions; they are God's gift:** You and I are made in the image of God. As His image-bearers, we must learn to accept who we are. Our emotions step from our values and what we believe in. What do you believe in? Are you conforming yourself to the image of Christ? The Bible says in John 3:30, "He must increase, but I must decrease." As we become more like Christ, our thoughts, values, and actions conform to His image. We start to view the world through God's eyes. This is why praying for God's

will daily and surrendering to Him is vital. This is how we are transformed, little by little, by the renewal of our minds.

2. **Learn to label your emotions:** Talk Therapy is something therapists use to help patients deal with their negative feelings. When you talk about how you feel or the events of your life, you will be able to let them out of your system. Have you ever spoken to a friend about your troubles and felt better? You let yourself feel and process the emotion when you learn to talk it out and share it with someone. There may be days when the pain runs so deep that you cannot find the right words even to describe it. At times such as this, run to the Word of God. The words in the book of Psalm, Proverbs, and Lamentations will help you and soothe your soul. The Psalmist says in Psalm 118:14, "The LORD is my strength and my defense; he has become my salvation." In times of trouble, run to God. He is your refuge (Psalm 46). Generally, learning how to label and express your emotions can be very healthy and free. Share it with a trusted friend or partner and see how it starts to lift.

3. **Grow in the love of God:** When you become a believer, you start to notice the love of God. Paul says in Ephesians 3:17-18, "Your roots will grow down into God's love and keep you strong. And may you have the power to understand, as all God's people should, how wide, how long, how high, and how deep his love is." His love makes us strong. God is always and eternally the same; He never changes. But as we grow deeper into Him, we start to notice how amazing His love is. This profound awareness changes how we feel, think and process our emotions. Growing in His love is beautiful and life-changing.

Master your emotions with God by your side:

Here are a few common emotions we deal with daily. Let us also look at what the Bible has to say about them:

1. **Depression:** Depression is painful. It can be caused by

chemical imbalances, dire circumstances, rejection, or isolation. The Biblical characters who struggled with depression are David, Elijah, and Moses. God worked miracles and wonders in the lives of these people. He dearly and deeply loved them. He was always with them, even in their darkest despair. If you're struggling with depression, I want you to know that you are not alone. There is hope and a great future because God holds you (Jeremiah 29:11).

A few Bible verses to strengthen you are:

- Psalm 46
- Deuteronomy 31:8
- Psalm 34:17
- Isaiah 41:10
- Psalm 40:1-3
- John 16:33
- Romans 8:38-39
- 2 Corinthians 1:3-4
- Matthew 11:28

2. **Fear, Anxiety, Stress, and Worry:** These emotions are rooted in fear and uncertainty. After Jesus's death, His disciples lived in fear and locked themselves in a room (John 20:19). They were stressed, worried, and in fear because their master had been taken away from them. But after the resurrection, Jesus came to meet them, and He sent His Holy Spirit, who is always with us. I want you to remember that God is always with you. He walks with you, talks to you, and cherishes you.

Here are a few verses to fight these emotions:

- 1 John 4:18
- Psalm 27:1
- Isaiah 41:10

- Matthew 6:25-26
- Proverbs 3:5-6
- Philippians 4:6-7
- Psalm 55:22
- 1 John 4:18
- Psalm 23:4

3. **Loneliness:** Loneliness is a very common occurrence and leads to other disorders like depression, insomnia, and substance abuse. Many Biblical prophets suffered from loneliness. Paul struggled with loneliness, and we see this in 2 Timothy 4:16-17, where he says, "At my first defense, no one came to my support, but everyone deserted me. May it not be held against them. But the Lord stood at my side and gave me strength." Many times, we are surrounded by people, yet we feel alone. Jesus struggled with loneliness, too (Isaiah 53:5). Take courage, dear friend. God is with you. He never left Paul's side, and He won't leave yours. You are not alone; the Lord is your Shepherd. If it gets too overwhelming, I urge you to talk to a close friend, your spouse, or your church pastor. Ask for prayer.

Verses to help you fight the attacks of the enemy:

- Psalm 27:9-10
- Isaiah 58:11
- Galatians 6:2
- Psalm 102:5-7; 18-20
- Hebrews 4:15-16

4. **Doubt:** The enemy is very good at sowing seeds of doubt in our minds. He makes us doubt our salvation, relationships (both with God and humans), and sanity. Fight these doubts with the Word of God. Fight them with His promises. Gideon struggled with doubt and tested the Lord

three times (Judges 6,7). Remember that you have the sword of the Spirit and use it to slay the devil.

Here are a few promises that God gave His children:

- Romans 10:12-13
- Genesis 18:14
- Mark 9:24
- Matthew 14:30-31
- Matthew 21:21-22
- Proverbs 3:5-6

5. **Guilt:** Guilt is rooted in either conviction or self-condemnation. When you sin, God convicts you of it and calls you to repentance. When God forgives you, learn to forgive yourself. Unfortunately, the devil often feeds your mind lies and tells you that you are still guilty. You must learn to fight his lies with the truth of the Word.

Here are a few verses to help you deal with guilt:

- Hebrews 10:22
- Psalm 32:1-2
- Romans 8:1
- Psalm 103:12
- Romans 3:22-24
- I John 2:1
- Hebrews 8:12

6. **Insecurity:** Insecurity is rooted in a negative self-image. Often, it springs from awful childhood experiences or other traumatizing events. Insecurity can destroy you. You bear the image of God, and your identity lies in Him. Your past or your circumstances do not define you. You fight insecurity by knowing and claiming your identity in Christ. You are a child of God (Ephesians 1:4-6).

Here are a few verses to root yourself in:

- Romans 8:31-32
- 1 John 1:3
- 1 john 4:16
- 1 Corinthians 6:11
- Matthew 10:29-31
- Psalm 139:13-14

7. **Frustration:** Frustration leads to anger and bitterness. When swimming against the tide, it is hard not to be bitter. But, as we found in Christ, we must remind ourselves of His goodness. The prophet Jeremiah was frustrated and wrote the lamentations in his bitterness. But he chooses to trust in God even through his weary circumstances. When you feel like you've hit a wall and had your fill, I encourage you to read the book of Psalms.

A few verses to fight frustration are:

- Romans 8:28
- John 16:33
- Ecclesiastes 3:1
- Philippians 4:6-7
- James 1:2-4
- Psalm 37:4-5

8. **Inferiority:** If you struggle with the feeling of inferiority, know that you are precious and worthy in God's eyes. Jesus called fishermen and tax collectors to be his disciples. He always has a way of using the weak and making them strong.

Here are a few verses that will strengthen you:

- 1 Corinthians 1:26-29

- Jeremiah 1:5
- Galatians 3:28
- Job 12:3

You have the power to choose:

God has given you the gift of free will, and no matter what you tell yourself, you have the power to choose. You can choose the way to react to situations. Bob Proctor once said, "When you react, you are giving away your power. When you respond, you are staying in control of yourself." The power to exercise self-discipline lies in you (2 Timothy 1:7). Choose to respond to a thought or a situation rather than jumping to a conclusion. How do I exercise this right?

- **Our Emotions usually react:** Emotions can be frustrating at times, but once you learn to exercise self-discipline and self-control by bringing these emotions under Christ's control, you will learn to respond rather than react.
- **Our Minds evaluate:** Feed your mind with the Word of God. When our minds are filled with His truth, we can battle any lie.
- **Our Wills choose:** Choose to be better. Choose to grow in Christ. Your free will is a gift, but you will be held accountable for exercising it correctly. Use God's Word as your weapon of choice so that you grow into Him.

7

FINDING GOD IN TIMES OF CRISIS

"Whatever happens, conduct yourselves in a manner worthy of the gospel of Christ."

— PHILIPPIANS 1:27

The coronavirus pandemic was unlike anything we have ever experienced and has left many of us devastated. The uncertainty and fear that piled up almost covered normalcy. The news was filled with sad stories and the days kept passing without measure, and, to top this all off, isolation was the new normal. How can we not worry about our health or finances during days like this? Yet, I'd be lying if I said I wasn't attacked by fear during the pandemic.

Saints like Ignatius of Loyola encourage us 'to find God in all things,' yet moments like these make us wonder if God really does care about us. Where is God in the pandemic? As the Switchfoot song, *Vice Verses*, goes, "Where is God in the earthquake? Where is God in the genocide? Where are you in my broken heart? Everything seems to fall apart." Is God absent in pain?

These questions seem to trigger anxiety and doubt within me. What is the answer to these questions, though? God is always with us (Psalm 118:6), in the earthquake, in the genocide, and especially throughout the pandemic. Psalm 34:18 says, "The LORD is close to the brokenhearted and saves those who are crushed in spirit." He is with you in your days of pain, and The Bible says that He is very close to those who are in pain. The God of comfort never leaves us (2 Corinthians 1:3).

We often reach a boiling point where things get way out of hand, and we become utterly helpless. We do everything in our strength to work things out according to God's Word, we try to be wise, yet the storm hits us like a tsunami. The Bible talks about this in Psalms 107:27-29, "They reeled and staggered like drunkards; they were at their wits' end. Then they cried out to the Lord in their trouble, and he brought them out of their distress. He stilled the storm to a whisper; the waves of the sea were hushed." Some circumstances push us to the edge, but look at what the second half of the verse says. When they cried out to God, He brought them out of trouble and calmed the storm. This is who God is; faithful and able to save. Whatever your circumstance, know that there will be victory!

The 'Whatever happens' mindset:

Paul says in Philippians 1:27, "Whatever happens, conduct yourselves in a manner worthy of the gospel of Christ." Paul was writing this to the Philippians from a Roman prison. The context here was that he was supposed to visit them, but the circumstances seemed against this, and he wasn't sure of it happening anytime soon. So, he commanded the Philippians to conduct themselves in a way that is worthy of the Gospel even if he didn't make it. What is the lesson we learn here? Whether in the presence or absence of good circumstances, we must live lives worthy of the Gospel. Our circumstances do not matter; our devotion to Christ does.

That seems a bit too harsh and impractical, but how do we live up to such high standards? The answer is *grace.* The Bible says in Titus 2:11-12, "For the grace of God has appeared that offers salvation to all people. It teaches us to say "No" to ungodliness and worldly passions and to live self-controlled, upright, and godly lives in this present age." God's grace has been poured out onto us in a supernatural measure, which is how we will make it. We have the Holy Spirit dwelling in us; He is our helper and guide (Romans 8:26-27).

Jesus came to die. The Bible says in 1 Timothy 1:15, "Here is a trustworthy saying that deserves full acceptance: Christ Jesus came into the world to save sinners—of whom I am the worst." He came to be sacrificed for us. He knew it from the beginning and willingly died for you and me. Jesus had the perfect attitude; there was no sin in Him (1 Peter 2:2). He prayed about everything and constantly desired and did the will of the Father (John 5:19). Even when He was subjected to great suffering, He did not open His mouth and complain (Isaiah 53:7). Christ endured so that we may be saved forever. He knew what would happen to Him, yet He came down in complete humility and obedience (to the Father).

Whatever your circumstance is today, know that you get through it. Set your mind on heavenly things (Colossians 3:12). Fix your eyes on the author and perfector of your faith (Hebrews 12:2). Surrender to His will. When you try to control the people around you, your future, or even your circumstances, you are trying to take the place of God. Instead of fighting in your strength, pray the Psalm 5:8, which says, "Lead me, Lord, in your righteousness because of my enemies—make your way straight before me." With God by your side, you are an overcomer!

Selflessness, righteousness, and hope do not come naturally during testing times. Why? Because we are flesh and blood. But, as children of God, it is possible to cultivate the 'Whatever happens' mindset by leaning into faith. Faith is what pleases God (Hebrews 11:16). Tap into the ever-flowing reserves that God gives His children. As you walk through each trial, God works on your sanctification and stretching your faith. We cannot expect a plant to grow without any effort. A seed dies and gives up its contents to give rise to a new plant. It is a process that doesn't happen overnight. Testing times are excruciating but good.

In the book of Daniel, we see that King Nebuchadnezzar made an image of gold and demanded that all people worship it (Daniel 3:5). Shadrach, Meshach, and Abednego refused to bow down to this idol. As the story goes on, the king threatens to throw them into a fiery furnace as punishment for their disobedience. But this was their reply, "Our God whom we serve is able to deliver us from the burning fiery furnace, and he will deliver us out of your hand, O king. But if not, be it known to you, O king, that we will not serve your gods or worship the golden image that you have set up (Daniel 3:17-18)." The consequence of disobedience was death, yet these men chose to trust in God and die for their faith. They decided to praise God and give Him all the glory even when there seemed to be no hope. This was a "Whatever happens' situation.

Nebuchadnezzar was furious and ordered his soldiers to make the furnace seven times hotter than the average temperature. The furnace heat was so high that the soldiers responsible for throwing the three men into the fire were killed by the heat. But the good news is that this wasn't the end of their story. There was another in the fire which protected them from the blazing fire. The three men came out untouched; the Bible says that not even a hair on their heads was touched. This is great faith, friend.

King David was at his wits' end:

It is believed that David was 15 years old when the prophet Samuel anointed him to become king over Israel. Saul was ruling over Israel at that time, but God's Spirit had departed from him as the Lord had rejected him as king. David waited a long time to see the promise come to life. He waited around 13 years before he became the king of Israel. David faced many trials and tribulations before he saw the promise of God come to pass. His life was filled with many ups and downs, and his faith was tested many times.

The people of Israel started to praise and favor David over Saul, which led to Saul developing feelings of jealousy and hatred. After a particular battle, the people of Israel celebrated the victory and sang, "Saul has slain his thousands, and David his tens of thousands " (1 Samuel 18:7)." So, Saul wanted to kill David. When he came to know about Saul's murderous rage, David ran away.

Saul received reports of David visiting the high priest at Nob (1 Samuel 22). He interrogated the priests' company and found out that they had given David the bread from the tabernacle. Saul was enraged at this and ordered the priests to be slaughtered. David came to know of this and was deeply distressed. At the same time, David received news of Samuel's death (1 Samuel 25:1). However, Samuel was an intercessor and prayed over David, and as long as he was alive, David had a prayer covering him. To top this off, Saul learned about David's hiding place in the Judean wilderness (1 Samuel 26). David was utterly exhausted.

We then notice that David did something bizarre. He left his homeland and went to the land of the Philistines (1 Samuel 27:1). He probably reasoned that Saul would not attack him there and so went on to live in enemy territory. David was facing a severe spiritual crisis. It seemed that he had started to lose his faith. Everything around him turned against him. What would you do in such circumstances? Would you hold onto God or give up?

One day, after another battle, David and his men returned home to Ziklag to find that their families had been taken away by the Amalekites (1 Samuel 30). Their houses were burnt to the ground. All the men were utterly distressed and blamed David for it. They wanted to stone him for it. Do you see how David's circumstances kept getting worse? David lost everything. This was rock bottom; it couldn't get any worse. At this point, he decided to run to the Lord and enquire about His will. David asked God, "Shall I pursue this raiding party? Will I overtake them?" God told him to go ahead and pursue them.

During this situation, we see that David strengthened himself in the Lord (1 Samuel 30:6). When we study this situation, we see that David surrendered everything to God. He ran to God and made Him his refuge. David knew God was not done with him; his promise still stood firm. God was going to accomplish much through David. So, take refuge in God when you are at your wits' end and cannot go on anymore. He will strengthen you and uphold you with His righteous right hand (Isaiah 41:10).

When you have no strength, God will give you supernatural strength. David and his army started pursuing the Amalekites and found a sick Egyptian on the way. The raiding party abandoned this man. David asked the man about the plans of the Amalekites, and he spilled the beans. He told them the Amelekites' entire battle plan. David and his men won the battle and recovered everything. This is an excellent example of God's provision. God was setting up David for a fantastic victory!

There will be times when you've lost everything, and you feel nothing is left. But God will strengthen you and lead you in His strength. He will provide for you and take care of your every need. God always makes a way where there is no way. So when you think that all hope is lost, remember that God is working for your good behind the scenes (1 Corinthians 10:13). There will be victory here!

Leaning into faith during testing times:

Exercising our faith during testing times is vital. The Bible says in James 1:2-3, "Consider it all joy, my brethren, when you encounter various trials, knowing that the testing of your faith produces endurance." All these trials will result in us conforming more and more to the image of Christ. Our goal is to become more like Him with every passing day. Here are a few ways by which you can practically exercise your faith:

1. **Examine what you feel in your heart:** Everything we do comes from our hearts (Proverbs 4:3). What is the condition of your heart? Is your heart set on the King? Or are you distracted by the worries of life? The Psalmist says in Psalm 139:23-24, "Search me, God, and know my heart; test me and know my anxious thoughts. See if there is any offensive way in me, and lead me in the way everlasting." He asks God to check His heart. The Bible also says that what defiles a man comes from within the heart (Matthew 15). Your actions will be driven by what is in your heart, which is your heart's direction. Take some time to ask God to check your heart. Invite the Holy Spirit to come and reveal the condition of your heart. Ask Him to lead you in the way everlasting (in God's will).

2. **Meditate on the Word of God:** Meditating on God's word must become a habit. His word will strengthen us and lead us through the most challenging situations in life. The Bible says in Joshua 1:8, "Keep this Book of the Law always on your lips; meditate on it day and night, so that you may be careful to do everything written in it. Then you will be prosperous." God speaks to us primarily through His word, which is why we must develop the habit of reading it every day. When you learn to fix your eyes on God actively, your focus will change. You will become more sensitive to what He says and dwell on His promises rather than your pain.
3. **Pray in challenging situations:** The Bible asks us to pray without ceasing (1 Thessalonians 5:17). Paul also commands us to "pray in the Spirit on all occasions with all kinds of prayers and requests. With this in mind, be alert and always keep on praying for all the Lord's people (Ephesians 6:18)." Prayer is one of our greatest weapons. Before you pray, forgive those who have sinned against you because unforgiveness can hinder your prayers. There are days when we don't know how to pray. During such times, the Holy Spirit intercedes for us and helps us pray (Romans 8:26-27). Prayer doesn't have to be complex; it is simply you talking to your Father.
4. **Renew your mind:** We've seen this concept repeatedly. Renewing your mind begins by surrendering to God completely. For example, Joseph was sold into slavery by his brothers. Years later, we know he meets his family when they come to Egypt for food. After the death of his

Father, his brothers are scared that he will want revenge. But Joseph replies, "As for you, you meant evil against me, but God meant it for good, to bring it about that many people should be kept alive, as they are today (Genesis 50:20)." God renewed Joseph's mind. I'm sure he'd be filled with bitterness and rage if God didn't restore his heart. When you focus on what God says, your mind will pursue His Words. When you focus on your anxiety or pain, you're giving in to the lies of the devil.

5. **Be on the lookout for the unexpected ways God might be working in the crisis (build up your faith):** God tends to surprise us. The Bible says in Romans 8:28 that *all* things work out for good for those who love God. So, your faith is being tested when you walk through the valley. It would help if you reminded yourself of this eternal promise. Paul says in Hebrews 11:1, "Now faith is confidence in what we hope for and assurance about what we do not see." Faith knows that God has already secured His promise to you; it is just a matter of time until it comes to pass. Remember that anything is possible with God (Luke 1:37).

6. **Offer praise to help you cope:** Did you know that praise puts the devil in his place? Before the wall of Jericho fell, the Lord commanded Joshua and the Israelites to march around the wall with trumpets and shouts of praise seven times (Joshua 6). After they marched around and shouted praise to God, the walls of Jericho came crashing down. Praise always goes before the battle is won. We are claiming our victory in Christ and reminding the devil of the fact that he is defeated. Seasons come

and seasons go, but God is eternally faithful. When you feel low, put on the garment of praise and see the darkness disappear (Isaiah 61:3).

7. **Refocus on the important things of life:** I want you to think of the things of utmost importance to you. Is it your family? Is it your spouse? As believers, God is our ultimate goal. He is and must always be our number 1. When Jesus visited the home of Mary and Martha, Martha was distracted by all the preparations. In contrast, Mary was sitting at Jesus' feet and listening to Him (Luke 10:40). She then complained to the Lord about her sister Mary. To this, the Lord said, Martha, Martha, you are worried and upset about many things, but few things are needed—or indeed only one. Mary has chosen what is better, and it will not be taken away from her." God corrected her and drew her attention to the 'one thing' she needed. Are you distracted by the other things in life? Has God taken a back seat in your life? If yes, then you need to make some changes. Think about this and examine yourself.

8. **Connect with close people around you:** Human beings were not made to be alone. We were made to commune with others and enjoy their company. Unfortunately, the recent pandemic has pushed us into isolation. Isolation isn't good for our hearts. It breeds anxiety and depression in quite a few cases. With technology, it is easy to keep in touch with loved ones. It is vital to ensure that you take care of your mental health during times of crisis. To love and be loved is what the human soul longs for. Human connection can make all the difference on hard days when you just need someone to talk to.

9. **Take care of your spirit, soul, and body:** Self-care is essential. The world defines self-care in terms of the soul and body, but we define self-care as the body, soul, and spirit. Our spirits need nourishment. Do you know that you can be sick in your spirit? Unconfessed sin can lead to spiritual sickness. Have you been taking care of your spirit? Have you been open and accountable to God in all that you do? If there is any hidden or unconfessed sin, I urge you to confess it and ask God for forgiveness. Sickness in the spirit can manifest itself as mental and physical sickness too. It is essential to take care of your soul too. Always remember that Jesus is the Prince of Peace and our healer. He bore all your sickness on the cross and in His name so you can be healed. Take care of your soul and body too!

Prayer to come back to yourself:

God called you to His glorious light; you are His. If you think you have wandered away from Him, come back home. He is waiting for you with arms wide open. He is faithful and will leave the 100 for the one. Come home. Pray this prayer with me:

"You are God.

I praise you because you are holy and worthy of it all.

I thank you for dwelling in my heart.

I thank you for making me Your child.

I thank you for working in my life.

You guided me into salvation, renewed my dead spirit, and opened my eyes to the Truth.

You know my pain and suffering,

Nothing about my life is hidden from you.

Heal me and make me whole, God.
Saturate me with Your presence.
Bring me back to you, Lord.
Thank you."

"'If you can't?" said Jesus. "Everything is possible for one who believes"- Mark 9:23

8

CULTIVATING GODLY GRATITUDE

"For where your treasure is, there your heart will be also."

— MATTHEW 6:21

C.S. Lewis once said, "We ought to give thanks for all fortune: if it is good because it is good, if bad because it works in us patience, humility and the contempt of this world and the hope of our eternal country." I love how he beautifully explained that, as citizens of an eternal country, it all works out for good (Romans 8:28). When our times are good, God is good. When our times are bad, God works out our sanctification, and He is still good! This is because our faith lies in God's character, not our changing circumstances. He is eternal and unchanging (Hebrews 13:8). His love endures forever (Psalm 136).

One of my favorite verses is 2 Timothy 2:11-13, which says, "If we died with him, we will also live with him; if we endure, we will also reign with him. If we disown him, he will also disown us; if we are faithless, He remains faithful, for he cannot disown himself." So we give thanks to God because we will forever live with Him; we give thanks because we will reign with Him forever and ever. We give Him thanks because He will never leave us; He is faithful—gratitude springs from having faith in an eternal God.

A lot of times, we fail to count our blessings and thereby succumb to bitterness and grumbling. The Bible says in James 1:17, "Every good and perfect gift is from above, coming down from the Father of the heavenly lights, who does not change like shifting shadows." Pay attention to the language used here. The author says that *every* perfect gift, not just a few, is from the Father. Do you have a home to live in? It is a good gift from the Father. Do you have a wardrobe full of good clothes? It is a gift from the Father. Do you have good relationships with the people around you? These are all perfect gifts from our heavenly Father.

The power that comes with gratitude:

As we saw in the previous chapter, we always have a choice. We can choose to respond to a situation or immediately react to it. In our daily life, we can choose to feel either Inferior or Satisfied. We can tell ourselves that we're not 'good enough' or 'smart enough,' or we can choose to love who we are just the way God made us (in His image). We can grumble over not having enough in life or choose to appreciate all God has blessed us with.

We can choose to be overwhelmed with life, or we can trust God and place our confidence in His. We can choose to be depressed and moody, or we can choose to be happy and positive. Being happy and positive doesn't mean you deny reality; you decide to trust God's sovereignty. You can choose to victimize yourself by feeling sorry for yourself, or you can decide to stay in control of your past or circumstances. God has gifted us with a sound mind (2 Timothy 1:7) and a choice to think the right thoughts. It is up to us to decide what we dwell on.

The choice we make has the power to alter our reality. Do you know what the Bible has to say about grumbling or complaining? Philippians 2:14-15 says, "Do everything without grumbling or arguing, so that you may become blameless and pure, children of God without fault in a warped and crooked generation." We are asked to do *everything* without grumbling. Grumbling dishonors God; it is the antithesis of faith.

The Israelites grumbled and complained for years and years even when they kept seeing the goodness of God every single day (Exodus 17:4). Like the Israelites, we can choose to dwell on our circumstances and focus on all that we lack. We can wallow in self-pity and make ourselves helpless victims and blame those around us, or we can be grateful for all the good things in our life.

What does gratitude bring to your life?

The Bible says in Psalm 136:1, "Give thanks to the LORD, for he is good. His love endures forever." God's love is more significant than anything we will ever experience. We live, walk, and take being in His love. There are innumerable things to be grateful for, but how does gratitude benefit us? The benefits of practicing gratitude are:

1. **Gratitude grounds us in the present:** With the Coronavirus pandemic hitting the world, we've been forced to deal with many emotional issues. During such challenging times, we try to reminisce about the past or already start planning for the future. But what does the Bible have to say about this? The teacher says in Ecclesiastes 7:10, "Do not say, "Why were the old days better than these?" For it is not wise to ask such questions." Besides this,

Paul says that we are supposed to be thankful in ALL circumstances and at all times (1 Thessalonians 5:18). This is God's will for us. So, the next time you feel like thinking about the past or the future, know that God's will for you is to enjoy His gift of the present.

2. **Gratitude brings us back to our spiritual selves:** Gratitude shifts our focus from our circumstances or troubles to God. It brings us back to His image. When we thank Him for all He has done, our spirit rejoices. When you focus on what you lack, you give in to the enemy's trap. But when you focus on God, a river of gratitude flows from your heart. This is because we are spiritual beings, and our complete satisfaction and fulfillment lie in God alone.

3. **Gratitude brings peace:** The Bible says in Philippians 4:6-7, "Do not be anxious about anything, but in every situation, by prayer and petition, with thanksgiving, present your requests to God. And the peace of God, which transcends all understanding, will guard your hearts and your minds in Christ Jesus." Gratitude fights anxiety and stress. Every time you feel stressed, learn to count your blessings. The peace that God gives is not of this world, and it transcends all our futile efforts to gain it from worldly things. Jesus is the Prince of Peace (Isaiah 9:6).

4. **Gratitude nurtures contentment:** John Piper once said, "God is most glorified in us when we are most satisfied in Him." As spiritual beings, our nourishment comes from God alone. Paul was one of the most outstanding men ever to walk this earth. He left everything for Christ. He says in

Philippians 4:11-13, "I am not saying this because I am in need, for I have learned to be content whatever the circumstances. I know what it is to be in need, and I know what it is to have plenty. I have learned the secret of being content in any and every situation, whether well fed or hungry, whether living in plenty or want. I can do all this through him who gives me strength." Paul learned to be grateful and content in all circumstances. Oh, I only pray that the Lord would give me a measure of this man's faith. When we find our complete identity in Christ, we will choose to put our trust in Him. He will become our everything. How can we spend an eternity with Christ if we're not satisfied with Him? Ponder upon this question.

5. **Gratitude builds faith:** Gratitude is rooted in God's eternal providence. The Bible says in Philippians 4:19, "And this same God who takes care of me will supply all your needs from his glorious riches, which have been given to us in Christ Jesus." Here it says that God will supply *'all our needs,'* not our wants or wishes. Needs are for survival. The Lord knows how to take care of His children. He brought birds and rained manna from heaven to feed the Israelites (Exodus 16). You and I serve the same God; He is mighty and able to provide. He will take care of His children because we are His. Our faith increases with thanksgiving because our trust is rooted in Him.

6. **Gratitude fosters joy:** The joy of the Lord is our strength (Nehemiah 8:10). Joy springs from happiness and satisfaction. It is a fruit of the Spirit (Galatians 5:22-23). Jesus came to give us the oil of joy instead of mourning (Isaiah 61:3). Joy springs

from a grateful heart; it is like medication to the soul. As His children, joy is something we will receive because we trust in Him. Practice gratitude and His joy; it will keep you full.

Developing the Attitude of Gratitude:

Gratitude changes us. It changes our perspective, outlook, and feelings. It changes the way we think and express ourselves. It literally changes how we respond to situations. So making it a habit is crucial.

Now that we've seen the benefits of gratitude and what it is, let us look at some practical ways to develop this habit:

1. **Create a Gratitude List:** After your daily devotion, write down three things you are grateful for that specific day. Maybe it's your spouse or your children. Perhaps it's your family getting together for dinner. You can even maintain a gratitude journal to do this. Then, write down three things you're grateful for every single day, and remind yourself of them the following day. Sometimes, we don't realize what we have until we are asked to look at it.
2. **Look beyond your current circumstances:** Life is full of ups and downs, but God is constant and faithful through it all. If you're struggling with something today, know that God is for you (Romans 8:31), and He is holding you by His righteous right hand (Isaiah 41:10). He is faithful forever (Deuteronomy 7:9). There is hope for you. Fix your eyes on Him. Let Him stretch your imagination. Feed your faith because this is what pleases God.

3. **Create a daily ritual of gratitude:** As seen above, write down three things you're grateful for daily. Routines can be personalized based on what you like to do. For example, I usually journal daily and write a letter to God. In my letter, I tell Him what I did that day and the things that made me happy. I also thank Him for His goodness and mention what I'm grateful for. In the same way, find something you love and express your gratitude to God through it.
4. **Keep evidence of past gifts from God:** I have a box of things I collected from every place I've ever traveled to. These are my small joys. I cherish them, and they make me happy. In the same way, I journal things that have happened and promises of God that have come to pass. My heart leaps for joy every time I read one of these stories; these are my souvenirs. You can do the same. Maybe it's a mug, pen, notebook, or something that reminds you of God's goodness. Store these gifts as reminders of His love and faithfulness.
5. **Learn to be content at all times:** I know this is easier said than done. Learning to be content comes by exercising your faith and being completely satisfied with God. How do you do this? By appreciating the smallest of things around you. It's always the small joys! Over a while, these little joys pile up and lead to a mountain of happiness and fulfillment. Being content in God is knowing that He holds you no matter what.
6. **Pass it forward:** Jesus commanded us to love our neighbors as ourselves (Matthew 22:37-39). He also said in Matthew 25:40, "Truly I tell you, whatever you did for one of the least of these

brothers and sisters of mine, you did for me." Jesus served us to such an extent that He sacrificed His very life for us. In the same way, as children of God, we are called to serve others and help them in times of need. We are called to serve others. I urge you to read Isaiah 58, which talks of True Fasting that glorifies God and makes His heart glad. When you give to others, you pass God's love to them. You are a vessel of His love, which will bring you immense joy. You will understand how blessed you are, increasing your gratitude.

7. **Build your future on thanksgiving:** Building your future on thanksgiving will open doors of blessing that you never knew existed. As believers, we must strive to live in the center of God's will, and in this place dwells thanksgiving. Praise and thanksgiving (Psalm 100:4-5) condemn the enemy and weaken Him.

8. **Thank Him every time you pray:** Start your prayer by thanking the Lord for all that He has done. There is always something to be grateful for. The Bible says in Psalm 107:21-22, "Let them give thanks to the Lord for his unfailing love and his wonderful deeds for mankind. Let them sacrifice thank offerings and tell of his works with songs of joy." So give Him an offering of praise; exalt Him because He is worthy of it all.

What can you give thanks for?

Sometimes, we get so caught up in our messes that we fail to see the good in anything. We become bitter and angry. We start to blame others. Unfortunately, there are many consequences to being bitter. Bitterness is like a slow poison that suffocates your immune system and kills you painfully. It makes the heart grow sick. It drives you into negative thinking and traps you in an endless cycle. Did you know that bitterness affects metabolism, immune responses, and organ functioning? There are many chances of you developing physical diseases too.

If you've been struggling with unhealed wounds, bitterness, or constant anger, I urge you to list everything you're grateful for. Stick notes of these things around you. Keep reminding yourself of them. If you are unable to come up with a list, here are a few pointers:

1. **Begin each day by thanking God:** Let me give you a list of things to be thankful for:

- A new day
- Good health
- Family
- Freedom to read God's Word daily
- Being a child of God (salvation)
- Sleep/rest
- A good life

2. **Compliment generously:** The Bible says in Proverbs 17:23, "A cheerful heart is good medicine, but a crushed spirit dries up the bones." Happiness is contagious. When you compliment someone, you are giving them the gift of joy.

3. **Gratitude journal:** Maintaining a gratitude journal can be freeing. When you write down what you're grateful for, your mind starts to process it better. I know that not everyone is a writer, and you don't have to put much effort into this. Just write down the small things, the things that made you smile that particular day. Then, after a few years, you will jump and dance while reading this book.

4. **Smile, smile, smile:** Did you know that your brain

releases neurotransmitters that fight stress every time you smile? When you consciously practice positive emotions like being confident, happy, or grateful, your brain chemistry starts to change. Your brains get used to these emotions, and you become a new person. Smile more often because your heavenly Father loves you (1 John 4:6). He thinks good thoughts about you (Jeremiah 29:11). There are a million reasons to smile today; just look around you!

5. **Serve those in need (Volunteer):** We are called to serve others like Christ did (Philippians 2:4). Take time to volunteer at places that need help. Help those in need. Helping others is a great way to practice gratitude as it will remind you of Christ's love for you (and others).

6. **Gratitude jar:** Gratitude jars are usually visual reminders of one's blessings. Every time something good happens to you, or you see a promise fulfilled, write it down on paper and slip it into the jar. In this way, you can savor God's goodness and practice thankfulness.

7. **Thank God throughout the day:** Paul asks believers to pray without ceasing (1 Thessalonians 5:17). Praying throughout the day about small things can be very edifying. Thank the Lord for the smallest blessings and give Him the glory and praise He deserves.

8. **Prioritize spending time with loved ones:** Did you know that spending more time with your family can result in fewer behavioral problems? In addition, it leads to greater confidence among family members. Families are precious to God because they are the building blocks of love. When you spend more time with your family, you will start to see how much God has blessed you through them. As a result of this, you will overflow with gratitude to Him.

9. **Random acts of kindness:** God is kind (Ephesians 2:7). The Bible says in Galatians 6:9-10, "And let us not grow weary of doing good, for in due season we will reap if we do

not give up. So then, as we have the opportunity, let us do good to everyone, especially those of the household of faith." Kindness reflects the state of our hearts. If our hearts are filled with the love of God, compassion will overflow from them. Use small opportunities to be kind to others. Random acts of kindness will remind you of Christ's love for you. Out of His heart, He gave up everything for you.

10. **Practice controlling your thoughts:** We've seen many ways of doing this since the beginning of the book. In retrospection, have you started managing your thoughts and making them obedient to Christ?

11. **Take nature walks:** Nature is a gift of God to humankind. It is filled with His artistry and imagination. As you walk through nature, remind yourself of how beautiful God is. He is so good! His love never fails. The Bible says in Matthew 6:25-26, "Therefore I tell you, do not worry about your life, what you will eat or drink; or about your body, what you will wear. Is not life more than food, and the body more than clothes? Look at the birds of the air; they do not sow or reap or store away in barns, and yet your heavenly Father feeds them. Are you not much more valuable than they?" Remember this verse as you walk through God's creation. Surrender your worry to Him.

AFTERWORD

THE BEST IS YET TO COME

"The pain that you've been feeling can't compare to the joy that's coming."

— ROMANS 8:18

"For I know the plans I have for you," declares the Lord, "plans to prosper you and not to harm you, plans to give you hope and a future. Then you will call on me and come and pray to me, and I will listen to you. You will seek me and find me when you seek me with all your heart." -Jeremiah 29:11-13.

God wants what is best for you. The above promise is for all of His children. His Word is for you no matter your circumstance or what you are going through. Through this book, we have defined what toxic thoughts are and how to deal with them. We have seen the difference between complaining and venting. The books of Psalms and Lamen-

AFTERWORD

tations are filled with lament and sorrow. The book of Ecclesiastes grounds us.

If your situation is terrible today, I urge you to seek God today. Just because it seems bad now doesn't mean there is no hope. There is always hope in God's Word and promises. You have to work in cooperation with God; stand on the foundation of His many promises. Build your house on it. You are working with the devil if you work with your negative thoughts. Align yourself with God's Word today!

All thing will work for your good (Romans 8:28). Speak life over yourself! Speak God's truth over yourself. Once you start to believe that *all* things will work out for you, you will see that there is nothing to complain about. Count your blessings and find something to be grateful for today! If you think you are too far from God, fear not. Come to the altar. There is salvation here. Just come.

If you've enjoyed reading this book, please leave a review!
God bless you abundantly!

FREE GIFT

Just for you!

An enlightening ebook that will give you new revelation about the power of the Holy Communion! Download it right away!

Visit this link: unmeritedfavourllc.com

BIBLIOGRAPHY

1. Chapter 6, The Screwtape Letters: CS Lewis et al. "Chapter 6, The Screwtape Letters: CS Lewis". *Thespiritlife.Net*, 2021, https://www.thespiritlife.net/81-warfare/warfare-publications/1881-chapter-6-the-screwtape-letters-cs-lewis.
2. Bible Gateway Passage: Romans 12:2 - New International Version". *Bible Gateway*, 2021, https://www.biblegateway.com/passage/?search=Romans%2012%3A2&version=NIV.

"Romans 1:21- English Standard Version". *Biblehub.Com*, 2021, https://biblehub.com/romans/1-21.htm.

1. "2 Corinthians 5 NKJV". *Biblehub.Com*, 2021, https://biblehub.com/nkjv/2_corinthians/5.htm.
2. "Genesis 3:12 – English Standard Version". *Biblehub.Com*, 2021, https://biblehub.com/genesis/3-12.htm.
3. "Bible Gateway Passage: Matthew 11:28-30 - New International Version". *Bible Gateway*, 2021, https://www.biblegateway.com/passage/?search=Matthew%2011%3A28-30&version=NIV.
4. "Bible Gateway Passage: Lamentations 3:22-23 - English Standard Version". *Bible Gateway*, 2021, https://www.biblegateway.com/passage/?search=Lamentations%203%3A22-23&version=ESV.
5. "Bible Gateway Passage: Philippians 2:14-15 - English Standard Version". *Bible Gateway*, 2021, https://www.biblegateway.com/passage/?search=Philippians%202%3A14-15&version=ESV.

"2 Timothy 2:14 NIV". *Biblehub.Com*, 2021, https://biblehub.com/niv/2_timothy/2.htm.

BIBLIOGRAPHY

1. "1 Samuel 1 ESV". *Biblehub.Com*, 2021, https://biblehub.com/esv/1_samuel/1.htm.
2. "Genesis 16 NIV". *Biblehub.Com*, 2021, https://biblehub.com/niv/genesis/16.htm.
3. "Bible Gateway Passage: Jeremiah 29:11 - New International Version". *Bible Gateway*, 2021, https://www.biblegateway.com/passage/?search=Jeremiah%2029%3A11&version=NIV.
4. "Bible Gateway Passage: Proverbs 23:7 - New King James Version". *Bible Gateway*, 2021, https://www.biblegateway.com/passage/?search=Proverbs%2023%3A7&version=NKJV.
5. "Bible Gateway Passage: Ecclesiastes 11:9-10 - New International Version". *Bible Gateway*, 2021, https://www.biblegateway.com/passage/?search=Ecclesiastes%2011%3A9-10&version=NIV.
6. "Isaiah 30:15 (NIV)." *Bible Gateway*, www.biblegateway.com/passage/?search=Isaiah%2030%3A15&version=NIVAccessed 5 Oct. 2021.
7. "Psalm 139:13–14 (NIV)." *Bible Gateway*, www.biblegateway.com/passage/?search=Psalm%20139%3A13-14&version=NIV. Accessed 5 Oct. 2021.

"Ecclesiastes 1:13 ESV." *Bible Hub*, biblehub.com/esv/ecclesiastes/1.htm. Accessed 5 Oct. 2021.

1. "John 17:17 (NIV)." *Bible Gateway*, www.biblegateway.com/passage/?search=John%2017%3A17&version=NIV. Accessed 5 Oct. 2021.
2. "Romans 8:28 (NIV)." *Bible Gateway*, www.biblegateway.com/passage/?search=Romans%208%3A28&version=NIV. Accessed 5 Oct. 2021.
3. "Isaiah 49:15 (NIV)." *Bible Gateway*, www.biblegateway.com/passage/?search=Isaiah+49%3A15&version=NIV. Accessed 5 Oct. 2021.

BIBLIOGRAPHY

4. "Luke 17:6 (NIV)." *Bible Gateway*, www.biblegateway.com/passage/?search=Luke%2017%3A6&version=NIV. Accessed 5 Oct. 2021.

"Proverbs 4:23." *Biblestudytools.Com*, www.biblestudytools.com/ncv/proverbs/4-23.html. Accessed 5 Oct. 2021.

1. "1 Corinthians 1:18 (NIV)." *Bible Gateway*, www.biblegateway.com/passage/?search=1%20Corinthians%201%3A18&version=NIV. Accessed 5 Oct. 2021.
2. "Romans 8:26–27 (NIV)." *Bible Gateway*, www.biblegateway.com/passage/?search=Romans%208%3A26-27&version=NIV. Accessed 5 Oct. 2021.

"Ephesians 6:12 ESV." *Biblia*, biblia.com/bible/esv/ephesians/6/12. Accessed 5 Oct. 2021.

1. "2 Corinthians 10:3–5 (KJV)." *Bible Gateway*, www.biblegateway.com/passage/?search=2%20Corinthians%2010%3A3-5&version=KJV. Accessed 5 Oct. 2021.
2. "Proverbs 4:23–25=NCV - - Bible Gateway." *Bible Gateway*, www.biblegateway.com/passage/?search=Proverbs+4%3A23-25=NCV. Accessed 5 Oct. 2021.

"Isaiah 61." *Biblestudytools.Com*, www.biblestudytools.com/isaiah/61.html. Accessed 5 Oct. 2021.

1. Tozer, A. W. "Tozer Devotional | Our Infinite Worth in Christ." *The Alliance*, www.cmalliance.org/devotions/tozer?id=794. Accessed 5 Oct. 2021.
2. "Ruth 1:13 (NIV)." *Bible Gateway*, www.biblegateway.com/passage/?search=Ruth+1%3A13&version=NIV. Accessed 5 Oct. 2021.

BIBLIOGRAPHY

3. "Ruth 1:20–21 (NIV)." *Bible Gateway*, www.biblegateway.com/passage/?search=Ruth+1%3A20-21&version=NIV. Accessed 5 Oct. 2021.
4. "2 Corinthians 13:5 (KJV)." *Bible Gateway*, www.biblegateway.com/passage/?search=2+Corinthians+13%3A5&version=KJV. Accessed 5 Oct. 2021.

"John 8 NIV." *Bible Hub*, biblehub.com/niv/john/8.htm. Accessed 5 Oct. 2021.

1. "Isaiah 41:10 NIV" *Bible Hub*, biblehub.com/isaiah/41-10.htm. Accessed 5 Oct. 2021.
2. "Romans 5:20." *Bible Hub*, biblehub.com/romans/5-20.htm. Accessed 5 Oct. 2021.
3. "2 Corinthians 12:9 (NIV)." *Bible Gateway*, www.biblegateway.com/passage/?search=2%20Corinthians%2012%3A9&version=NIV'. Accessed 5 Oct. 2021.
4. "Our Thought Life - Jesus Lives." *Jesus Lives - A Grassroots Ministry*, 27 July 2021, jesuslives.com/our-thought-life.
5. "Isaiah 26:3 (NIV)." *Bible Gateway*, www.biblegateway.com/passage/?search=Isaiah%2026%3A3&version=NIV. Accessed 5 Oct. 2021.

"Psalm 119 NIV." *Bible Hub*, biblehub.com/niv/psalms/119.htm. Accessed 5 Oct. 2021.

1. "Romans 12 NIV." *Bible Hub*, biblehub.com/niv/romans/12.htm. Accessed 5 Oct. 2021.
2. Prince, Derek. "They Shall Expel Demons: What You Need to Know about Demons: Your Invisible Enemies by Derek Prince." *Good Reads*, Choosen Books, www.goodreads.com/book/show/164042.They_Shall_Expel_Demons. Accessed 5 Oct. 2021.
3. "2 Corinthians 10:5 (KJV)." *Bible Gateway*, www.biblegateway.com/passage/?search=2%20Corinthians%2010%3A3-5&version=KJV. Accessed 5 Oct. 2021.

BIBLIOGRAPHY

4. "Hebrews 12:1 (NIV)." *Bible Gateway*, www.biblegateway.com/passage/?search=Hebrews%2012%3A1&version=NIV. Accessed 5 Oct. 2021.
5. "Philippians 4:8 (NIV)." *Bible Gateway*, www.biblegateway.com/passage/?search=Philippians%204%3A8&version=NIV. Accessed 5 Oct. 2021.

"1 Kings 17:12." *Biblestudytools.Com*, www.biblestudytools.com/1-kings/17-12.html. Accessed 5 Oct. 2021.

1. "Isaiah 41:10 (NIV)." *Bible Gateway*, www.biblegateway.com/passage/?search=Isaiah%2041%3A10&version=NIV. Accessed 5 Oct. 2021.

"1 Kings 17:14." *Bible Hub*, biblehub.com/1_kings/17-14.htm. Accessed 5 Oct. 2021.

1. "1 Kings 18:1 NIV." *Bible Hub*, biblehub.com/niv/1_kings/18-1.htm. Accessed 5 Oct. 2021.
2. "Romans 12:2 (NIV)." *Bible Gateway*, www.biblegateway.com/passage/?search=Romans%2012%3A2&version=NIV. Accessed 5 Oct. 2021.

"Matthew 7:21." *Bible Hub*, biblehub.com/matthew/7-21.htm. Accessed 5 Oct. 2021.

1. "Philippians 3:13–14 (NIV)." *Bible Gateway*, www.biblegateway.com/passage/?search=Philippians%203%3A13-14&version=NIV. Accessed 5 Oct. 2021.
2. "Philippians 4:6–7 (NIV)." *Bible Gateway*, www.biblegateway.com/passage/?search=Philippians+4%3A6-7&version=NIV. Accessed 5 Oct. 2021.

"Psalm 119:11 (NIV)." *Bible Hub*, biblehub.com/niv/psalms/119.htm. Accessed 5 Oct. 2021.

BIBLIOGRAPHY

1. "Colossians 3:2–4 ESV." *Biblia*, biblia.com/bible/esv/colossians/3/2-4. Accessed 5 Oct. 2021.
2. "2 Corinthians 4 KJV." *Bible Hub*, biblehub.com/kjv/2_-corinthians/4.htm. Accessed 5 Oct. 2021.
3. "Romans 12:21 (NIV)." *Bible Gateway*, www.biblegateway.com/passage/?search=Romans%2012%3A21&version=NIV. Accessed 5 Oct. 2021.
4. "1 Corinthians 11:1 (NIV)." *Bible Gateway*, www.biblegateway.com/passage/?search=1%20Corinthians%2011:1&version=NIV. Accessed 5 Oct. 2021.
5. "Matthew 17:20 (NIV)." *Bible Gateway*, www.biblegateway.com/passage/?search=Matthew%2017%3A20&version=NIV. Accessed 5 Oct. 2021.
6. "Philippians 4:7 (NIV)." *Bible Gateway*, www.biblegateway.com/passage/?search=Philippians%204%3A7&version=NIV. Accessed 5 Oct. 2021.
7. "Matthew 10:30–31 (NIV)." *Bible Gateway*, www.biblegateway.com/passage/?search=Matthew%2010%3A30-31&version=NIV. Accessed 5 Oct. 2021.
8. "Psalm 94:19 (NIV)." *Bible Gateway*, www.biblegateway.com/passage/?search=Psalm%2094%3A19&version=NIV. Accessed 5 Oct. 2021.

"2 Corinthians 4 KJV." *Bible Hub*, biblehub.com/kjv/2_corinthians/4.htm. Accessed 5 Oct. 2021.

1. "Hebrews 4:12 (NIV)." *Bible Gateway*, www.biblegateway.com/passage/?search=hebrews+4%3A12&version=NIV. Accessed 5 Oct. 2021.

"Proverbs 4 New American Standard Bible." *Bible Hub*, biblehub.com/nasb_/proverbs/4.htm. Accessed 5 Oct. 2021.

BIBLIOGRAPHY

1. Piper, John. "Quote." *SermonQuotes*, sermonquotes.com/profound/15407-until-you-know-that-life-is-war-you-cannot-know-what-life-is-for-john-piper.html.
2. "Matthew 14:29–31=NIV - - Bible Gateway." *Bible Gateway*, www.biblegateway.com/passage/?search=Matthew+14:29–31=NIV. Accessed 5 Oct. 2021.
3. Elliot, Elisabeth. "A Quote by Elisabeth Elliot." *Good Reads*, www.goodreads.com/quotes/801197-we-want-to-avoid-suffering-death-sin-ashes-but-we. Accessed 5 Oct. 2021.
4. "Jeremiah 17:9 (NIV)." *Bible Gateway*, www.biblegateway.com/passage/?search=Jeremiah%2017%3A9&version=NIV. Accessed 5 Oct. 2021.
5. Puri, Ravinder. "Mindfulness as a Stress Buster in Organizational Set Up." International Journal of Education and Management Studies, vol. 5, no. 4, Indian Association of Health, Research and Welfare, Dec. 2015, p. 366.
6. "John 11:33–35=NIV - - Bible Gateway." *Bible Gateway*, www.biblegateway.com/passage/?search=John+11%3A33-35=NIV. Accessed 5 Oct. 2021.

"Psalm 103 NIV." *Bible Hub*, biblehub.com/niv/psalms/103.htm. Accessed 5 Oct. 2021.

1. "1 John 3:1." *Bible Hub*, www.biblehub.com/1_john/3-1.htm. Accessed 5 Oct. 2021.
2. "Proverbs 13:20 (NIV)." *Bible Gateway*, www.biblegateway.com/passage/?search=Proverbs%2013%3A20&version=NIV. Accessed 5 Oct. 2021.

"Ephesians 6 NIV." *Bible Hub*, biblehub.com/niv/ephesians/6.htm. Accessed 5 Oct. 2021.

1. "Hebrews 4:12" *Bible Gateway*, www.biblegateway.com/passage/?search=Hebrews%204%3A12&version=NIV. Accessed 5 Oct. 2021.

BIBLIOGRAPHY

2. "Ephesians 6:14–16 (NIV)." *Bible Gateway*, www.biblegateway.com/passage/?search=Ephesians%206%3A14-16&version=NIV. Accessed 5 Oct. 2021.

"Proverbs 15 NLT." *Bible Hub*, biblehub.com/nlt/proverbs/15.htm. Accessed 5 Oct. 2021.

1. "Psalm 101 ESV." *Bible Hub*, biblehub.com/esv/psalms/101.htm. Accessed 5 Oct. 2021.
2. "James 1:22–25 (NIV)." *Bible Gateway*, www.biblegateway.com/passage/?search=James%201%3A22-25&version=NIV. Accessed 5 Oct. 2021.

"Matthew 22 NIV." *Bible Hub*, biblehub.com/niv/matthew/22.htm. Accessed 5 Oct. 2021.

1. "Galatians 5:22–23 (NIV)." *Bible Gateway*, www.biblegateway.com/passage/?search=Galatians%205%3A22-23&version=NIV. Accessed 5 Oct. 2021.
2. "Proverbs 17:22 (NASB)." *Bible Gateway*, www.biblegateway.com/passage/?search=Proverbs%2017:22&version=NASB. Accessed 5 Oct. 2021.

"Emotion." *The Merriam-Webster.Com Dictionary*, www.merriam-webster.com/dictionary/emotion. Accessed 5 Oct. 2021.

1. "Proverbs 26:4–5 (NIV)." *Bible Gateway*, www.biblegateway.com/passage/?search=Proverbs%2026%3A4-5&version=NIV. Accessed 5 Oct. 2021.
2. "John 3:30 (NIV)." *Bible Gateway*, www.biblegateway.com/passage/?search=john+3%3A30&version=NIV. Accessed 5 Oct. 2021.

"Psalm 118 NIV." *Bible Hub*, biblehub.com/niv/psalms/118.htm. Accessed 5 Oct. 2021.

BIBLIOGRAPHY

1. "Ephesians 3:17–19 (NLT)." *Bible Gateway*, www.biblegateway.com/passage/?search=Ephesians%203%3A17-19&version=NLT. Accessed 5 Oct. 2021.
2. "2 Timothy 4:16–17 (NIV)." *Bible Gateway*, www.biblegateway.com/passage/?search=2%20Timothy%204%3A16-17&version=NIV. Accessed 5 Oct. 2021.
3. Proctor, Bob. "Respond with Intention." *A Quote by Bob Proctor*, www.cindrakamphoff.com/428-2-2-2-2-2-2-2-2-2-2-2-2-2-2-2-2-2.
4. "Matthew 6:21 (NIV)." *Bible Gateway*, www.biblegateway.com/passage/?search=Matthew%206%3A21&version=NIV. Accessed 5 Oct. 2021.

Lewis, C. S. "C. S. Lewis Quote." *A-Z Quotes*, www.azquotes.com/quote/779531. Accessed 5 Oct. 2021.

1. "2 Timothy 2:11–13 (NIV)." *Bible Gateway*, www.biblegateway.com/passage/?search=2%20Timothy%202%3A11-13&version=NIV. Accessed 5 Oct. 2021.
2. "James 1:17 (NIV)." *Bible Gateway*, www.biblegateway.com/passage/?search=James%201%3A17&version=NIV. Accessed 5 Oct. 2021.

"Philippians 2:15." *Bible Hub*, biblehub.com/philippians/2-15.htm. Accessed 5 Oct. 2021.

1. "Psalm 136:1 (NIV)." *Bible Gateway*, www.biblegateway.com/passage/?search=Psalm%20136%3A1&version=NIV. Accessed 5 Oct. 2021.

"Ecclesiastes 7:10 NIV." *Bible Hub*, biblehub.com/niv/ecclesiastes/7.htm. Accessed 5 Oct. 2021.

BIBLIOGRAPHY

1. "Philippians 4:6-7." *Bible Gateway*, www.biblegateway.com/passage/?search=Philippians%204%3A6-7&version=NIV. Accessed 5 Oct. 2021.
2. "Philippians 4:11–13 (NIV)." *Bible Gateway*, www.biblegateway.com/passage/?search=Philippians+4%3A11-13&version=NIV. Accessed 5 Oct. 2021.

"Philippians 4:19." *Bible Hub*, biblehub.com/philippians/4-19.htm. Accessed 5 Oct. 2021.

1. "Matthew 25:40 (ESV)." *Bible Gateway*, www.biblegateway.com/passage/?search=matthew+25%3A40&version=ESV. Accessed 5 Oct. 2021.
2. 101."Psalm 107:21–22." *Biblestudytools.Com*, www.biblestudytools.com/psalms/passage/?q=psalm+107:21–43. Accessed 5 Oct. 2021.

"Galatians 6:9–20 ESV." *Bible Hub*, biblehub.com/esv/galatians/6.htm. Accessed 5 Oct. 2021.

1. 102."Matthew 6:25–26 NIV." *Bible Portal*, bibleportal.com/verse/-therefore-i-tell-you-do-not-worry-about-your-life-what-you-will-eat-or-dri-niv-7599. Accessed 5 Oct. 2021.
2. 104."Philippians 1:27 (NIV)." *Bible Gateway*, www.biblegateway.com/passage/?search=Philippians%201%3A27&version=NIV. Accessed 5 Oct. 2021.
3. 105."Psalm 107:27–28 (NIV)." *Bible Gateway*, www.biblegateway.com/passage/?search=Psalm%20107%3A27-28&version=NIV. Accessed 5 Oct. 2021.

"Titus 2:12 NIV." *Bible Hub*, biblehub.com/niv/titus/2-12.htm. Accessed 5 Oct. 2021.

BIBLIOGRAPHY

1. 106."1 Timothy 1:16 (NIV)." *Bible Gateway*, www.biblegateway.com/passage/?search=1%20Timothy%201%3A16&version=NIV. Accessed 5 Oct. 2021.

"Daniel 3:17–18." *Bible.Com*, www.bible.com/bible/compare/DAN.3.17-18. Accessed 5 Oct. 2021.

1. 108."1 Samuel 18:7 (NIV)." *Bible Gateway*, www.biblegateway.com/passage/?search=1%20Samuel%2018%3A7&version=NIV. Accessed 5 Oct. 2021.
2. 110."Psalm 139:23–24 (NIV)." *Bible Gateway*, www.biblegateway.com/passage/?search=Psalm%20139%3A23-24&version=NIV. Accessed 5 Oct. 2021.
3. 111."Joshua 1:8 (NIV)." *Bible Gateway*, www.biblegateway.com/passage/?search=Joshua+1%3A8&version=NIV. Accessed 5 Oct. 2021.

"Ephesians 6:18." *Bible Hub*, biblehub.com/ephesians/6-18.htm. Accessed 5 Oct. 2021.

1. 112."Genesis 50:20 ESV." *Bible Hub*, biblehub.com/esv/genesis/50.htm. Accessed 5 Oct. 2021.
2. 113."Luke 10:42." *Bible Hub*, biblehub.com/luke/10-42.htm. Accessed 5 Oct. 2021.
3. 114."Mark 9:23 NIV." *Bible Hub*, biblehub.com/niv/mark/9.htm. Accessed 5 Oct. 2021.
4. 115."Romans 8:18." *Bible Hub*, biblehub.com/niv/romans/8-18.htm. Accessed 5 Oct. 2021.
5. 116."Jeremiah 29:11–13 (NIV)." *Bible Gateway*, www.biblegateway.com/passage/?search=Jeremiah%2029%3A11-13&version=NIV. Accessed 5 Oct. 2021.

www.ingramcontent.com/pod-product-compliance
Ingram Content Group UK Ltd.
Pitfield, Milton Keynes, MK11 3LW, UK
UKHW021903240426
12048UKWH00038B/1260

9 798215 675250